Helping Vulnerable Children and Adolescents to Stay Safe

Helping Vulnerable Children and Adolescents to Stay Safe

Creative Ideas and Activities for Building Protective Behaviours

Katie Wrench

Foreword by Ginger Kadlec

Jessica Kingsley *Publishers*
London and Philadelphia

First published in 2016
by Jessica Kingsley Publishers
73 Collier Street
London N1 9BE, UK
and
400 Market Street, Suite 400
Philadelphia, PA 19106, USA

www.jkp.com

Library of Congress Cataloging in Publication Data
A CIP catalog record for this book is available from the Library of Congress

British Library Cataloguing in Publication Data
A CIP catalogue record for this book is available from the British Library

ISBN 978 1 84905 676 2
eISBN 978 1 78450 183 9

Printed and bound in Great Britain

Contents

Foreword

'My favorite color is red,' the small five-year-old confidently stated, his deep chestnut eyes smiling.

Whew. This sweet child was opening up to me as we chatted face-to-face in overstuffed blue chairs. One brother and two sisters before him had started to feel comfortable and safe in the same chair into which this tiny boy was now settling. They shared their favorite games, classes in school, music and more...but each stopped in their tracks when I transitioned the conversation to inquire, 'Are you worried about your mum?'

Countless child forensic interviews have left me scratching my head, wondering how someone could ever put a child through such atrocities. There are a few interviews, though, that haunt me to this day. This was one of them.

Earlier that day, the four children had witnessed their mother's rape and attempted strangulation at the hands of her boyfriend. The police responded, took statements, arrested the boyfriend and brought the mother and children to the community's child advocacy center so the traumatised kids could participate in forensic interviews to better determine what they had witnessed.

I asked the tiny boy about his mother – his lips tightened as his large eyes overflowed. Handing him a tissue, I knew we were done. He would disclose nothing to me that night...or ever. Sometime that afternoon, his mother decided she didn't want to press charges against her boyfriend. She had also convinced each of her children they would be taken from her and placed in separate foster homes if they disclosed anything about the incident earlier that day...and who knows? Or, perhaps about other violent incidents they had either witnessed or experienced themselves.

The very next day, the mother packed their belongings and followed her abusive boyfriend out-of-state with her vulnerable children in tow.

This case haunts me as I will never know if those children are safe. I can only hope their mother eventually found the strength and courage to escape an abusive situation in which far too many families find themselves trapped. Tragically, it's the children who ultimately pay the price.

Child forensic interviews and investigations into allegations of child abuse are only the beginning for victims. The real work of healing a child and his or her family comes as they participate in therapy and mend both surface wounds, as well as ones that are deeply rooted, and they develop the skills they need to ask for help when they need it and to keep safe in the future.

The global epidemic of child maltreatment assumes many forms. Children around the world are abused in both vicious and subtle manners ranging from sexual or physical abuse, to neglect, to psychological abuse; sadly, polyvictimisation is common among maltreated children. In the world of child abuse investigations and child forensic interviewing, there is a well-known fact:

Disclosure is a process, not a one-time event.

As is the case with abuse itself, disclosure can also take on many forms. It is common for children to 'test the waters' and share partial disclosures to assess how a person with whom the child is placing his or her trust will respond. Will the disclosure be met with doubt or hostility…or will it be received with immediate acceptance and reassurance? The manner in which a disclosure is received can literally make or break a child's decision to ever talk about the abuse again. The latter can lead to tragic consequences including further victimisation of the child, and possibly of others, as well as future mental or physical health problems such as self-injurious behavior, anxiety, depression, obesity and even suicide.

Disclosure can also assume the form of sudden outbursts or can be seen in a child's behavior and activity or even lack thereof – disclosure doesn't always present itself in the form of words or language one can readily comprehend. Herein lies the challenge for workers supporting vulnerable children and young people. The journeys of disclosure and healing for child abuse survivors are different for everyone; however, they do share some common traits.

In this book, *Helping Vulnerable Children and Adolescents to Stay Safe*, Katie Wrench affirms that the journeys of disclosure, healing and keeping safe are just that – journeys. Survivors don't complete their voyage in a single step, but rather travel a daunting, arduous path often filled with hazards and danger. That path, though, can be smoothed with respect, encouragement and a learned ability to self-protect. That's where you come in.

Katie outlines exercises and creative ideas that align with practices employed in child forensic interviewing protocol and basic body safety education methodology. Maintaining a 'Child First' philosophy whereby the child's needs are paramount, this book underscores the importance of rebuilding (or in some cases, constructing for the first time) a child victim's self-esteem, resilience and sense of safety as an integral part of the therapeutic process.

Utilising secrets, seizing moments of vulnerability or opportunity, and grooming targeted victims are common modus operandi of abusers and sexual predators. Katie presents methods to combat child maltreatment by helping the child build a sense of self, level of confidence and general understanding of personal boundaries and rights…all outcomes professionals involved in safeguarding vulnerable children hope to see.

As a child advocate, I applaud Katie for sharing valuable insight and tactical advice for social workers, therapists and counselors who are accompanying child survivors of abuse on their journeys. I also hope that these creative techniques will support workers to empower vulnerable children and adolescents to avoid repeat victimisation. I also thank YOU, the reader, for your commitment to strengthen and evolve your own professional methods and techniques to help children safely navigate and explore their own uncharted journeys of feeling safe, disclosure and healing.

Ginger Kadlec
Founder, BeAKidsHero™ *(http://www.beakidshero.com)*
Creator of the Sexual Abuse Prevention System™
(http://sexualabusepreventionsystem.com)
Indianapolis, Indiana, USA

Acknowledgements

It's been a tough year in many respects to be starting a new project like this, and on my own this time. A great inspiration has been the vitality and expertise of my team in Leeds – the Therapeutic Social Work Team – and the will from within the city to live by the mantra of 'child-friendly Leeds'. For us to do this, we have to put our most vulnerable children first, and I hope this book will help us in that quest.

Now is the time for the very big 'thank yous'.

To Steve Jones at Jessica Kingsley Publishers, for being so kind as to ask me to think about writing again, and to the team who then brought the book into being.

To Alison Ferguson (again) for her expert perusal of my drafts, for making my sentence structure less cumbersome and eliminating the self-doubting 'mights'.

To Lesley Naylor for reading through the activities with a clinical eye, making sure that my tone is friendly and that I haven't missed anything too obvious!

To Sarah Langli for talking through the issues around child sexual exploitation with me, and helping me form the outline of the chapter around how to work with vulnerable adolescents; and to Jan Hext for passing on her research around online safety.

To Stephen Giles for once again taking up the child care mantel – for spending days out with Louis and Honor to give me time to think and write. I know my mood hasn't always been wonderful, especially as the deadline has approached, but I couldn't have done it without you. My final thanks go to Honor for help with the wonderful 'working agreement'.

Thank you.

Introduction[1]

As a therapeutic social worker and art psychotherapist working with vulnerable children and young people, their parents and carers, I am often asked for advice and resources to support the development of protective behaviours and an understanding of how to help children keep safe. In recent years there have been various programmes aimed at promoting children's safety and protection from sexual abuse, such as the UK child protection charity National Society for the Prevention of Cruelty to Children (NSPCC) campaign promoting 'The underwear rule' (NSPCC no date).

The NSPCC encourages us to talk about 'PANTS':

Privates are private.

Always remember your body belongs to you.

No means no.

Talk about secrets that upset you.

Speak up, someone can help.

For the mainstream population of children, these are such valuable lessons. However, in my experience, for children who have already been victimised or who, for diverse reasons, may be vulnerable to victimisation, the issues are more complex. But what if you have been

---

1   Please note that throughout this book, for simplicity of reading and writing, I refer to children and young people using masculine pronouns as it can feel somewhat cumbersome to be repeatedly reading his/her, he/she, etc. Please take no meaning from this, and know that throughout I am talking about girls and boys here in equal measure. Where there are specific gender differences, I will make reference to these as appropriate.

threatened with death if you speak up? What if you spoke up and were not believed? What if you said 'no' and were repeatedly abused anyway? What if you can't remember the last time your privates were private? What if countless adults have used your body for entertainment or pleasure? What if you don't know whether a secret feels good or bad?

It is important to note here that although we can all agree that everyone has the right to feel safe all of the time, statistics across the globe tell a very different story. Over the past 20 years we have seen an increase in awareness regarding the safety of children and adolescents. We now know that children are more likely to be harmed by someone they know than by a stranger. In the UK in 2013/14 all four countries saw a sharp increase in reported sexual offences against children to the highest number (36,000) over the past decade (Jutte *et al.* 2015, p.26). In the US, more than 3 million reports of child abuse are made every year involving more than 6 million children (Childhelp no date). This, of course, only reflects the number of *reported* offences rather than *actual* total offences against children during that period. In Australia, 31 per cent of adults said they wouldn't necessarily believe a child who disclosed abuse (Protective Behaviours Consultancy Group of NSW no date). These are horrifying statistics.

There are many reasons why children may be more vulnerable to engaging in problematic sexual behaviours towards others or why certain children may be more vulnerable to experiencing exploitation or harm themselves. I summarise US psychologist Toni Cavanagh Johnson's thinking here (1998a, p.2), who highlights those children and young people who:

- may not have been appropriately supervised by adults
- may have lived in homes where sexual boundaries lacked clarity
- may have been exposed to pornographic material or adult sexual activity
- may have lived in environments where sex has been linked with violence
- may have experienced physical or emotional abuse or neglect
- may have experienced sexual harm – either directly or indirectly

- may have been forced to engage in sexual acts with another child or young person.

The NSPCC has also identified characteristics in children that might make them more vulnerable to exploitation or to being targeted or groomed for sexual abuse (Atkinson and Truan no date). They assert a sex offender may be more likely to target a child who is:

- too trusting
- seeking love or affection
- lonely or bereaved
- lacking in confidence
- bullied
- disabled or unable to communicate well
- in care or living away from home
- already a victim of abuse
- eager to succeed in activities such as sport, school or other interests that may allow them to be manipulated by a potential abuser.

Choosing a victim is rarely a random act. Sex offenders gain contact with children in diverse ways and will often go to great lengths to get close to children, to build trust and attach to their families, perhaps by offering to babysit or to take the child out for special treats. They may also take up positions in a school or in a caring profession that will give them easier access to children, for example, as a leader of a youth group or sports team. There are also obvious public places such as skate parks, playgrounds, swimming pools and around schools, where it is easier to get to know children. This is before we stop to consider the implications of growing online threats to children's safety.

While there are some common-sense rules for parents and carers to follow that build on good parenting skills and knowledge of their child, what I have come to realise in recent years is that while there are many manuals and small booklets about the protective behaviours model available (see, for example, Dawson no date; Geisler 2014; Golding and Todd 1994; Gordon 1995; Lippett 1990;

Schonveld and Myko 1999), most are aimed at mainstream education staff and consist primarily of lesson plans or group work activities.

This model was developed in the 1970s in the US by social worker Peg Flandreau West, and the initial emphasis was on school-based programmes with two major themes used to introduce protective behaviours:

- We all have the right to feel safe all the time.

- Nothing is so awful we can't talk to someone about it.

Although it has been adapted for many settings and developed further in Australia where Peg West lived and worked from 1985, in my experience, when social workers, therapists, foster carers or parents want to work with children who have already been victimised, who have a history of trauma and ruptured attachments or who have additional vulnerabilities around keeping safe, there are no dedicated resources for support.

As a result, not enough of this vital work takes place in a way that connects for the children and young people in relation to their complex trauma and attachment histories. This is not necessarily due to a lack of understanding of the importance of the work, but rather a lack of expertise and confidence from frontline workers, parents and carers.

From this place comes this book. I have developed this brief, easily accessible guide that will support professionals, parents and carers to involve children and young people in engaging, creative activities that will support them to better integrate messages around keeping safe. Although by no means an expert in the field, I have also included some basic principles around online safety primarily for parents and carers, as this is a growing area of concern. This is an evolving field, and there continues to be new information to support us – in Chapter 7 and in 'Help and Support' I've included some useful links to online sources to stay up to date with reliable advice on online safety.

We don't always have as much time as we might like to spend planning direct work sessions and gathering together resources, which is where I hope this guide will help. Throughout my 20 years supporting vulnerable children and adolescents as a residential care officer, social worker, foster carer and art psychotherapist, I have developed a tried and tested portfolio of ideas and activities.

In addition to this, I have researched all the relevant literature and endeavoured to adapt, where possible, ideas that might be found in other publications or manuals, so you don't have to. Where this is the case, I direct you to further reading.

The uniqueness of this book is the opportunity to access a range of activities all in one place, simply categorised, to enable you to easily identify those that will be suitable for working individually (or with adaptations in groups) with a range of children and young people. You will be able to do this without requiring extensive resources and without years of training as a therapist. You will also be able to apply many of the activities to other direct work scenarios in social work or therapy settings.

Each activity is clearly formatted and outlines the materials you will need, together with the process and aims of the activity, so that you and the child will be clear what you are working on. I have also added a 'Handy hints' section at the end of each activity to share my experiences of what has worked well for me, and potential pitfalls to look out for. Where appropriate, I offer ideas for extension activities, or alternative applications of the activity.

I encourage you to be creative and to use yourself in the work, while holding in mind the aims and objectives of the sessions. Always consider the individual child's needs and his developmental age and stage, and tailor the activity accordingly. Many of the activities can be adapted for young children, older adolescents and children with developmental delay or disabilities. Make use of the child's systemic network in your planning to identify suitable activities. Some can be completed in 30 minutes or less, while others may take two sessions. I offer a range of ideas in each area of the work so you can always have a 'Plan B'.

Be respectful of the time the children need, knowing that strong feelings, difficult memories or new disclosures about abuse to themselves or others may be triggered by this work. It is for this reason that you must be absolutely clear about your agency's policies and procedures around managing disclosures and safeguarding before you begin this work.

Disclosures can come at any time…usually when you are least expecting them, and most often in my experience during car journeys, at meal times or bedtime. With hindsight I realise now that I didn't always give the most helpful responses in the moment to children who shared their experiences with me, especially in my early career working in a children's home. There were many reasons for this; my naiveté and inexperience, shock or even sometimes my own distress were certainly factors. So I offer you some suggestions that might help both you and the child feel safer in the moment (see, for example, Martin 2007, p.28):

- Try your best to stay calm, or at least control your expressions of panic and shock. Be aware of how the child might be feeling and be ready to help him manage any distress or anxiety. Remember that even if it is distressing to talk about, sometimes children experience relief when abuse is spoken about openly for the first time. Your initial response is very important.

- Always, as your default position, believe the child. Children very rarely lie about abuse, and many will have been discouraged from disclosing by being told no one will believe them. Let the child know he is believed.

- Be clear about what the child is telling you to be sure you have understood properly. Record it in written form with information about date, time and context.

- Do your utmost to reassure the child the abuse was not his fault. You might say things like, 'You are so brave and so right to tell me about this', 'I'm sorry this happened to you and it isn't your fault' or 'How clever of you to remember to tell someone in your network' (see *Establishing Personal Networks* on page 64). This is a message that will need repeating many times before the child will begin to be able to integrate it, but it is a starting point for removing any sense of blame or shame from the child.

- Don't pressure the child for more detail or information – if a police investigation ensues for example, he will have to re-tell this story many times. In my experience it is not uncommon for children to drip-feed you parts of their story – testing out your response before sharing the full story. Are you able to tolerate it? Do you still like the child even though you know this new information about him? Will you believe the child? Not all the information will necessarily be shared in one conversation, and that's okay.

- It's really important not to put pressure on children to say more. Use their language and go at their pace.

- Listen attentively and ask only open-ended questions. Remember, that unless you are a police officer reading this, you are not investigating the allegation. Examples of open questions might be:

  - Tell me a bit more about that…

  - Where did this happen?

  - What did the person say/do?

  - How many times has this happened?

  - How do you feel when this happens?

- Don't promise to keep the disclosure secret. You simply can't do this. Talk to the child about who needs to know and how they will be told.

- Tell the child you are pleased he was able to tell you.

- Recognise that such conversations have an impact on you as a worker/parent/carer, and if possible, de-brief with a colleague, friend or partner after the session. Liaise with the appropriate professionals thereafter depending on your organisational context and in line with safeguarding procedures (see, for example, McElvaney 2016).

Any conversations around keeping safe cannot be complete without emphasising the importance of preventative, educative work. The benefits of supporting children and young people to integrate messages around keeping safe and protective behaviours are too many to list, but here are my priorities:

- development of self-esteem and resilience

- development of lifelong skills such as self-confidence, assertiveness, communication and problem-solving

- supporting children to make their own decisions rather than relying on being told what to do by others

- decrease in vulnerable children becoming victims of abuse or entering into harmful interpersonal relationships – they learn the skills they need to help them feel safe, together with the ability to get help when they need it.

Of course it must be acknowledged that, for some children, this sort of intervention around keeping safe may be the tip of a very large iceberg and will never be a substitute for longer-term therapeutic interventions that will support recovery from trauma and abuse. Please also seek this help for the child where appropriate, and liaise throughout with the child's carers or parents if they are not directly involved in the work to monitor the child's emotional wellbeing.

Children's thoughts and feelings about past abuse can often overwhelm their ability to integrate their experiences, make meaning from them and move on. It is these experiences that may drive current behaviours in negative or self-defeating ways and lead them into situations where they need help to feel and keep safe.

To begin to create a sense of safety for the child in your work, I would strongly recommend that you first create a 'working agreement' together.

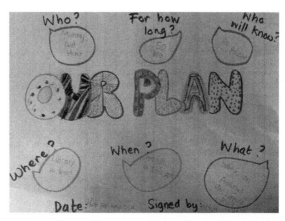

An example of a working agreement with an eight-year-old girl

You'll only need basic resources for this, such as drawing paper and pens. Other collage materials such as coloured paper, glue, stickers and glitter are nice to have, but not essential. The working agreement becomes a document that sets the ground rules for your sessions with the child and the child's parent/carer. There are no limits to how creative you can both be in this task, and I usually try to incorporate some of the child's interests within the image. For example, you could use a sporting theme, nature, pop or movie stars. The child might like to contribute his own ideas about the work, such as playing a quick game at the beginning of the sessions, or agreeing a way of letting you know when he needs a break. This is especially important for children or young people who have already been victimised and might feel anxious about not being able to control the process. They can sometimes be reassured by hearing you ask, 'How will you let me know if you need a break?' Or, 'How will you tell me if you feel unsafe or don't want to talk about something?'

The agreement should include key information for the child about what to expect from the work, including practical arrangements such as where and when you will meet, and how many sessions you will have together, and for how long. This is also the time to talk about confidentiality and the limitations of information boundaries. You will need to agree whom you will discuss the work with, such as the child's parent or carer if they are not in the session with you. The child may need to know where his parent/carer is during the session, if they're not going to be part of the work. Children and young people need to know that the process is confidential and that you will respect their personal histories. Be explicit about when you would break confidentiality – that safety concerns will always be prioritised over concerns about confidentiality. Also be mindful of requirements for child witnesses as part of any criminal proceedings, and apply the relevant guidance.[2]

Be clear about touch boundaries too. It is really important that children and young people are able to control when and how they are touched. Even social rituals such as shaking hands on meeting might need some thought. Similarly, you will need to ensure your own comfort zone is not infringed during the work. You might also include on the agreement that you will make sure the child is safe in the session and that you won't allow him to damage the room or equipment.

I encourage the child to sign the working agreement along with me, so there is a sense of shared ownership and understanding, although

---

2   See cps.gov.uk for the relevant guidance.

keeping the boundaries of time, space, materials and safety is always the adult's responsibility. In later sessions you will be able to come back to the document or image if the child is struggling to remember the rules. Some children will have a lot to contribute to the agreement, and you must be careful not to promise something that you can't deliver. Above all, you cannot guarantee to maintain confidentiality in all situations, as you will be working within safeguarding procedures and cannot predict what the child may disclose. I find that telling the child that you will discuss together anything you plan to let others know is reasonable (see, for example, Wrench and Naylor 2013, pp.27–28).

You might also want to think about some 'getting to know you' activities before you get started on the work proper. Sharing positive or creative experiences with a child is usually a good way of breaking the ice, but similarly a simple game of Hangman, Jenga or Noughts and Crosses can work just as well. Some ideas might include:

- A 'Getting to Know You' collage: You could use materials including photographs, images downloaded from the internet, magazines and craft materials. You could suggest co-creating a shared image, model or collage of 'safe' things about yourselves. A visually impaired child could make a collage with tactile connections to safety.

- An 'All About Me' badge: Make a badge with the child to share information about each other. Have a circle that you can divide into sections – for example, something I like to do, something I am good at, something I need help with, something I'd like to work on, something that is special to me, something about how I look, the name of a good friend, something that makes me happy, etc. You could also make a 'Me Tree' displaying the child's interests, likes and dislikes on branches and leaves (Lippett 1990, p.10).

- The 'All About Me' game produced by Barnardo's (no date) follows the familiar format of a colourful board game with dice and counters to take children on a path of discovery through feelings they may find difficult to express or deal with.

Finally, where this book does overlap with Peg West's work is that it is similarly presented as a 'web of ideas and strategies that feed and support each other; a process as much as (or more than) a program with lists and formulas; a process that stays within the individual's own control' (Gordon 1995, p.19). Please use the book fluidly and creatively, always holding in your mind how you will ensure that the work you undertake will have the greatest positive impact for the child or young person.

How we support vulnerable children to build protective behaviours and the length of time it takes for them to be integrated will vary greatly according to the child's age, developmental stage and previous experiences. There may also be times, no matter how well the child applies the strategies he has learned, that he may still be abused. People who are intent on grooming often use such sophisticated strategies to gain access to children that it remains key for adults to be ultimately responsible for safeguarding. We cannot expect children to be responsible for their own safety, even though we can support them to build protective behaviours. 'Prevention programmes alone do not prevent child abuse. Children have a compelling need for love and attachment and are thus vulnerable to the abuse of power by adults, including those in a position of trust' (Schonveld and Myko 1999, p.5).

So while you cannot guarantee these strategies will be 100 per cent successful, you can play a vital role in helping to introduce the skills children need to minimise the risks and to practise them in a safe environment. We must support children to become more informed about where to find help when they most need it, to anticipate and plan for how they will manage threatening situations, and to become more connected with their feelings.

Please remember that it's not necessary to work through all the activities in this book in the order they are presented; indeed, there are countless overlaps and various activities that could serve different purposes at different times. You will need to assess for yourself and with the child's network how much focus each area will need depending on the child's individual needs and experiences. Much of the learning and integration will also take place between sessions, so make sure you equip the child's parent/carer to reinforce the work on a day-to-day basis. For each child and young person, consider whether it is appropriate for the parent/carer to be directly involved in the sessions, even if only as a witness.

A final note pertains to you, and managing your own feelings in this complex work, and your self-care. Just as you will be supporting young people to develop self-care and safety strategies, so must you develop these for yourself, and know when you need to put them into practice. Children and young people who have experienced trauma and abuse can unconsciously project their past experiences onto the present. Gender issues in the child–worker relationship can be relevant here, as can the worker's own behaviour or personal characteristics (e.g. hair colour, facial hair or perfume) that might elicit these projections or transference.

Transference is not always easy to spot; remember, above all, that these are emotional experiences that the child feels in response to you that he is unlikely to be able to explain or understand. It might be that in a positive sense you remind the child of a favourite neighbour and he will find himself feeling warm towards you. Or a child who has no trustworthy adult in his life may experience you as hostile or become suspicious of your motivation as you begin to get to know each other better. In essence, the child is transferring feelings about another person in his life to you. Noticing this can really help you to identify unmet needs in the child. These projections will have unique aspects for each child you work with depending on the perpetrator's gender, the child or young person's own sexual orientation and idiosyncratic aspects of any abuse experience. A solid understanding of the child's history is essential where possible to help you be aware of these possible issues.

Your wellbeing and integrity as a worker is fundamentally important. Use supervision to ensure your own life issues are not unconsciously played out with the children and young people with whom you work. Develop strategies to manage your own counter-transference – by this I mean what happens when your emotions are influenced by the child. Working with traumatised young people can elicit a powerful range of feelings in workers, and it's not unusual for you to develop your own defensive strategies that can sometimes mirror the child's during the work together, such as minimisation, avoidance or helplessness. I can think of children where I have routinely felt de-skilled and unable to influence their lives in any positive sense. I also recall other children where I have felt a sense of relief when a session has had to be cancelled.

Not all counter-transference is problematic, though. If you can learn to notice changes in your own emotional state during sessions, these cues can help reduce their possible negative impact on the dynamics of your relationships with the children and young people. You will be better able to differentiate what you need to deal with in supervision or personal therapy versus what is being raised in the session that is a clue to what the child might be feeling. For example, are there sessions with children that you dread, or do you feel overwhelmed by a certain child's issues? Do you notice that you are beginning to see a young person as 'special'? Are you stepping outside of your role or professional context to offer extra support or attention? Are you over-identifying with the child or are you minded to share specific personal information, perhaps because his experiences resonate with your own life experiences? These are all possible indicators of issues in the counter-transference to which you will need to pay attention.

In some circumstances it might be beneficial to engage in personal therapy to help you separate out your own processes from the child's; it is not uncommon for intersections to arise between our own personal histories and our professional lives. Know your own limits and personal boundaries, and be sure to have outlets outside of the workplace to enhance your own life experience, resilience and self-esteem. A balance between work and home is essential for good self-care; it can keep you energised and motivated as a worker. Whatever makes you feel good needs to be cultivated and supported, so make time for yourself.

Chapter 1

Building Resilience
and Self-esteem

Introduction

Adults cannot be with children every minute of every day to protect
them from harm. We cannot always prevent potential perpetrators
of harm approaching children, grooming them or even going on to
attempt to harm them. However, we can try to make our children
more challenging targets for victimisation. Kehoe writes:

> Children who feel good about themselves, who receive physical
> affection when needed, and who know that they are valued by
> their parents, are more likely to trust their own instincts in a
> stressful situation. Most importantly, they are also less apt to
> be manipulated by the 'special' or threatening aspects of the
> ongoing, abusive relationship. (1988, p.7)

It stands to reason that in working with children to keep safe, one
of our primary aims as workers, parents and carers is to boost the
child's resilience, which in turn then minimises risk factors. In relation
to more vulnerable populations of children, Brohl (1996, p.73)
reminds us that 'many children who have faced adversity not only
move beyond their trauma but seem to become stronger individuals.
This ability to thrive in the face of adversity, to overcome a traumatic
childhood, is called *resilience*.' Factors that encourage resilience can
be divided into two groups – individual and social – both of which

incorporate genetic and environmental components. With vulnerable children it is vital to identify the child's strengths as a starting point to building resilience. Whether it is considered an outcome, a process or a capacity, the essence of resilience:

> is a positive, adaptive response in the face of adversity. It is neither an immutable trait nor a resource that can be used up. On a biological level, resilience results in healthy development because it protects the developing brain and other organs from the disruptions produced by excessive activation of stress response systems. Stated simply, resilience transforms potentially *toxic* stress into *tolerable* stress. In the final analysis, resilience is rooted in both the physiology of adaptation and the experiences we provide for children that either promote or limit its development. (National Scientific Council on the Developing Child 2015, p.1; original emphasis)

The *individual factors* in the child that impact resilience include:

- Social competence: A range of social skills and the ability to make and keep friends.

- Temperament: All of us fit into one of these categories – easy, slow to warm, or difficult.

- Attractiveness: It's a social fact (albeit unpalatable for some) that children who are attractive or who have attractive features will be more popular with peers and adults.

- Sense of humour: Enables children to enjoy life and 'see the funny side', which can prevent disappointments or frustrations becoming overwhelming.

- Individual autonomy: A sense of having some control on a daily basis over what happens, while knowing they can rely on adults to guide them where needed.

- Intelligence: Important for problem-solving and thinking things through.

- Problem-solving: A range of skills to manage daily problems, help to understand options, choices and consequences, and to trust their judgement (see also Chapter 5).

- An ability to organise thinking and develop a coherent life story: Help to avoid the fragmented sense of self that often accompanies traumatic experience so that life makes sense (see Wrench and Naylor 2013).

- A sense of purpose and future: Small goals can build into bigger goals over time. Children need hopes and aspirations that are both achievable and realistic from a developmental perspective.

It is important across all aspects of a child's life that we look for opportunities to promote resilience, be it in school, through friendships, building social skills, leisure opportunities or through participation and responsibility. In terms of *social factors*, we are talking about the following areas:

- Friendships: Primarily, but not exclusively, with children of a similar age to share experiences together.

- Positive, secure relationships with adults: This could be parents/ carers or extended family members, teachers, sports coaches, religious leaders, etc.

- A strong sense of community: Belonging to and joining in a supportive extended community (e.g. religion, culture, sporting interest, etc.) can contribute to resilience.

- Family support: Families that can offer sensitive, supportive models of interpersonal relationships can act as a buffer against the challenges that life brings.

- Realistic and appropriate expectations: When children are struggling or vulnerable they shouldn't be set up to fail, but they should also have goals to reach for.

(Adapted from NSPCC 1977)

The other key concept we are working on in this part of the work is the child's self-esteem, a key building block of resilience (together with a secure base and self-efficacy). If self-esteem is the overall opinion we have of ourselves, many vulnerable children are likely to see themselves in a very poor light. The development of self-esteem begins in early childhood, and as Fennell writes:

Your ideas about yourself have developed as a consequence of your experiences in life. If your experiences have largely been positive and affirming, then your view of yourself is likely also to be positive and affirming. If, on the other hand, your experiences in life have largely been negative and undermining, then your view of yourself is likely to be negative and undermining. (2009, p.25)

It is so important for us to remember, however, that the development of a child's self-esteem is not an event but a process. 'Developing self-esteem is an inside job that requires outside help' (Grotsky, Camerer and Damiano 2000, p.69). It comprises many aspects of the child's self-worth, but also generally incorporates some comparison by the child between how he would like to be and how he thinks he measures up against this. The reality for children with low self-esteem is that they often feel powerless or incompetent, and can become isolated and fearful of new situations. Where children experience high levels of criticism, rejection or low parental warmth, they are left more vulnerable to approaches from people who seem on the surface to be offering much longed-for comfort and attention. Conversely, children with high self-esteem are generally more confident in dealing with difficult situations and seek help if they're in trouble. By valuing themselves, these children are less likely to be victimised or drawn into unhelpful or even harmful relationships.

So how might direct work with vulnerable children and young people build on personal and social resilient qualities?

- By offering the child activities and experiences that will bring pleasure and shared enjoyment. Games and activities can also reinforce essential problem-solving skills, while promoting *physical safety* (see also Chapter 5).

- By ensuring the child can observe and have evidence of the importance of his relationship with significant adults in his life, including parents/carers. The experience of feeling connected to another person (*attachment*) or belonging to someone or something is at the heart of learning about ourselves and about the world.

- By providing a containing and structured base from which the child can explore his experiences of safety. The presence of just one significant, predictable adult in a child's life is an important indicator for building resilience. For some this might be a family member, teacher, neighbour or sports coach. However, it might just be *you* who helps the child reframe any negative experiences and supports the development of resilience and *emotional safety* that will help him on his way to keeping safe in the future.

- By helping the child to notice the best things about himself and by having high hopes and expectations for him to *realise his possibilities*. Abused and traumatised children often grow up hearing negative stories about themselves, and hence have low expectations for life in the future. It can make a significant difference to a child's sense of self when someone articulates belief in him now and in who he might become in the future.

- By setting realistic age- and stage-appropriate expectations for behaviour and social interactions. Opportunities for teaching new behaviours should be managed in such a way as to *boost self-esteem* rather than humiliate or shame the child.

- By emphasising the positives in the child's life and in this work through *noticing the little things* he does well or tries hard to achieve, as well as 'the big stuff'.

Ultimately it is the everyday experiences children and young people have with parents/carers and teachers that provide the best opportunities for reinforcing self-esteem and building resilience, so you need to work hard with the child's systemic network to ensure this is happening as often as it should, through praise, encouragement and *affection*. These are the things that over time will help to create a core belief in a child and a felt sense that he is someone who is loveable and worthwhile. Children who feel this are typically more confident and secure. They are better able to manage stressors in their lives and to manage new situations or challenges with confidence, composure and hope.

Where children have impaired self-esteem and resilience, *achievement* – or 'the ability to transform ideas into actions' (Grotsky *et al.* 2000, p.71) – is also compromised. These children feel defeated before they have even begun. Children who have been shamed or humiliated become easily frustrated when things don't immediately go according to plan. Sometimes they worry they will be punished for failure. Bomber (2011, p.65) talks about teachers becoming 'human memory banks' for those children who are infinitely more likely to recall their struggles and failures than they are their successes. She also talks about children having 'multiple intelligences', and stresses the importance of exploring how children function best – 'learning' the child and his communication style. She references Pallett, Simmonds and Warman (2010, p.35), who describe multiple possible intelligences. For example, is the child *body smart* with good gross motor skills that make him successful in sports or dance? Is he *word smart* with the capacity to express himself verbally or learn new languages? Is he *art or music smart* with skills in performance or appreciation of music and art or skill with shape, colour or pattern? Is he *think smart* with great problem-solving skills or *number smart* with good mathematical or logical ability? Is he *feelings smart*, with a good understanding of his own needs and emotions? It's a sound reminder to explore *how* children are clever and successful.

Brohl has also developed a resiliency building checklist (1996, p.82), which looks at how to emphasise innate resilient qualities to reinforce positive coping skills and build self-esteem. I have adapted this here in order to offer some ideas of how to achieve this with children on a day-to-day basis as well as in direct work:

- Give the child special jobs or tasks appropriate to his level of competence and interests, and reward the efforts made towards completion rather than simply the end result.

- Notice and celebrate the child's sense of humour. Laugh with him.

- Support problem-solving skills and the development of self-efficacy (see also Chapter 5).

- Broaden the child's experiences through access to museums, the library, after-school activities, etc.

- Introduce a new hobby or skill to learn such as knitting, making a kite or paper aeroplane.

- Reinforce the child's skills by asking him to show you how he can, for example, kick a football, tie his shoelaces, sing a song or tell a joke.

What follows in this chapter are a range of activities that will help to tip the balance scale of child development towards positive outcomes for children and young people. They aim to boost self-esteem and resilience, and to support children to identify and express talents and strengths in themselves.

How I Make Myself Feel Better

I make no apologies for adapting this from *Life Story Work with Children Who Are Fostered and Adopted* (Wrench and Naylor 2013, pp.54–55), because I think it fits really well with trying to support children and young people think about the healthy strategies they have (or could develop with support) for feeling better when they are feeling vulnerable or unsafe.

Materials

Paper, felt tip pens, magazines or clipart/images downloaded from the internet (optional).

Process

Work together with the child to create a picture or list of what he does to make himself feel better when he feels things are not going so well. You might need to start by thinking about events, situations or people that help him feel bad, then move on to explore some of his solutions for helping himself at those times. When you discover something that soothes the child, record it in some way. Either ask him to write down or draw what he does or, if he prefers, you can write it down. If you have some prior knowledge of the child's self-care strategies, you might have prepared some clipart images that he could cut out to make a collage.

Depending on the list or image you develop together, you might want to go on to introduce new strategies he could use in future difficult situations. Ideas here could be to visualise his safe place (see *My Safe Place* on page 77), to go and find a trusted adult in his network (see *Establishing Personal Networks* on page 64), to write down or draw his feelings, to practise deep breathing or relaxation techniques (see *Relaxation Techniques* on page 80), to run around outside or bounce on the trampoline, to count to ten, or to listen to music or soak in a bubble bath.

Aims

- To identify and then build on the child's existing coping skills and to develop a wider repertoire of strategies.

- To raise the child's self-esteem and help him feel less powerless and more in control at times of difficulty or stress.

Handy hints

An adaptation of this activity comes from Tait and Wosu (2013, pp.164–166), with their 'comfort boxes'. They encourage the child to create a comfort box full of their favourite things, or things that bring them comfort. If you can't access the actual item or it is too big to fit in (e.g. a person or a pet!), you could draw a picture or use a photograph instead.

You may discover that some of the child's solutions for feeling better are not particularly helpful for him, for example, hitting out at others who have hurt him or swearing to release tension. For an older teenager this might also include having sex, smoking cigarettes, drinking alcohol or taking drugs. Try to identify at least one time when he chose a more helpful or pro-social way of managing, and really build on that. The aim is then to work with him to find new, healthier ways to feel better, and encourage him to practise them regularly. Check in with him during each future session to think about what has worked for him that week. If appropriate, think about ways in which to share these strategies with parents/carers and teachers so further encouragement can be provided at home and school to make good choices in difficult situations.

Strengths Based All About Me

Materials

A large sheet of drawing paper or wallpaper that the child can lie on, marker pen, felt tip pens/coloured pencils (other collage materials such as glitter, glue, stickers, coloured paper are optional).

Process

Ask the child to lie on the piece of paper and use a marker pen to draw round him, so that his body outline is on the paper. From here you can develop the image in many different ways. The child can make a self-portrait, deciding what clothes to wear, how to style his hair, etc. He can record important facts about himself around the drawing such as his birthday or place of birth, as well as what he likes and is good at. You could measure his height, weight or smile, and add that information to the picture, or ask how he would describe himself. If the parents/carers are present, they can also add positive comments or funny stories and anecdotes about the child. The outcome should be a colourful and informative image to represent the child as he is now, and a celebration of his strengths and achievements.

Aims

- To build a relationship with the child and learn something about who he is now, his likes and dislikes.

- To show your interest in the child and his world.

- To explore and build on the child's strengths and resilient qualities.

Handy hints

It may not be appropriate to draw around the child if he has been sexually abused or is uncomfortable with such close physical proximity to you. You may be better advised to draw a generic outline of a body, or ask the child to draw one, and use this in the same way. I have found it works well when the parent/carer is present as they can do the drawing instead of you, and can also contribute some lovely thoughts and memories of the child.

This activity can also connect with body awareness and boundaries (see Chapter 4) as the child can see a physical representation of himself – how tall he is, how much space he takes up – as well as working out the sorts of things that make him who he is.

Finding out what children like and dislike or their favourite things (colour, pet, TV programme, ice cream flavour, etc.) and what makes them special can also be done with worksheets. I often share some of my favourite things with the child too; for some children this is an important part of building up trust.

I'm the Greatest

Materials
None (although stickers or stars are optional).

Process
This is a great activity to do in a group – family, sibling or with other children. Have everyone sit in a circle so they can see each other. One at a time, each person will show off that they are 'the world's greatest' at something. They have about 30 seconds (you can time them for added fun) to share their story. Encourage the others to clap, cheer and whoop when the 30 seconds is up. Emphasise that they don't have to brag about something that they genuinely believe they're great at – allowing them to brag about anything at all helps encourage those who are shyer or who struggle to find the positives in themselves. For example:

'I'm the greatest singer!'

'I'm the greatest giggler in the world!'

'I'm the greatest at street dance!'

'I'm the greatest cake eater!'

'I'm the greatest dinosaur hunter!'

You can follow up with talking about how it felt to be 'bragging' – how did the others respond? You might offer a sticker or small prize to reward the telling, or you could write the successes on prepared stars to put up on the wall to share.

Aims

- To build on the child's self-esteem.

- To have some fun.

- To develop skills in relation to listening, giving and receiving praise.

Handy hints

This works well with young people when you have already done some preparatory work around building self-esteem and resilience; it may be helpful to reconnect with this work. There is a little book called *Tell Me About Your Greatness* (How 2013) that is lovely to use with younger children as a prompt; it is designed to teach children that their words and actions reflect their greatness. Another option for younger children aged 5–8 is *Marvellous Me* (Schwartz 1979), an 'all about me' book that celebrates the child's life and develops self-awareness.

An alternative is to encourage the child to talk about things that are true for him. This is a good way to share interests and to give and receive encouragement. In a group this could develop into an appreciation circle, where individuals share compliments with each other, such as:

'What I like about you is…'

'I enjoy doing…with you.'

You could also create a 'gallery' of images that celebrate the child's achievements. Remember, though, that an activity like this could easily tap into a child's low self-esteem if you don't offer support in noticing the positives. Be prepared and know that the very idea of celebrating self can be such a challenge for children with low self-worth or those who are immersed day-to-day in negative stories about themselves.

Feel Good Notebook

Materials

Pens and a notebook with collage materials and stickers for decoration.

Process

This is a great resource for any child or young person to help him focus on the positive experiences he has each day. We can all fall into the trap of focusing too much energy on everything that is going wrong on a given day or on the mistakes we have made. We forget about the simple good things that happen throughout the day. This could be making someone laugh, having fun at playtime or even having your favourite dessert after dinner.

Decorate the notebook using stickers, glitter and so on, to make it a reflection of the child's personality and what makes him feel happy and confident. Then suggest that each night the child takes a few minutes to write 5–10 good things that happened that day. If the child likes to draw, encourage him to draw a picture of one of the things he listed. If the child is too young to write, have him tell an adult about the positives from that day, or draw a picture and tell you or his parent/carer all about it. The key to this activity is consistency. This is a daily writing exercise to build a more positive view of the world.

Aims

- To build on the positives in the child's life.

- To build self-confidence and self-esteem.

- To provide evidence of successes or positive achievements.

Handy hints

Many young people like writing diaries, lyrics or poetry, so suggesting keeping a journal might be helpful. Adolescent diaries can 'provide an opportunity to disclose personal and intimate information. They can record reflections about, and emotional responses to, present and past personal experiences' (Geldard and Geldard 2004, p.158). This can be a useful link between your sessions and the adolescent's weekly experiences.

I also remember hearing from a foster carer who was having a really tough time caring for a risk-taking adolescent that she kept her own feel good notebook. Every time the young person did *anything* that was even vaguely positive, the foster carer recorded it in her notebook, even though at times it was very hard to catch this young person being good. At especially difficult times, she would re-read her notebook to remind herself of the strengths in their relationship, and would also share her notes with the young person.

Another foster carer has recently shared that she has started leaving a little note by her child's bed when she is sleeping, as a reminder of something that has gone well that day. The note is the first thing the little girl sees when she wakes, and she collects them in a little glass jar. When asked by her therapist how the notes make her feel, she simply replied, 'Awesome!'

The Tree

Materials

Pens and paper (a tree template with roots and branches is optional).

Process

This is an adaptation of an exercise from Tait and Wosu (2013, pp.85–86). You or the child draw an outline of a tree – make sure you have branches, a trunk and roots. Or you could use a pre-prepared template if you prefer. Talk about what the tree needs to survive – the roots take water from the soil to keep the tree alive and grow deep underground to anchor the tree and stop it from falling over in strong winds. A strong tree needs thick, sturdy, healthy roots that will carry on growing throughout the life of the tree, which adds to its safety and strength.

Then use this analogy to think about what the child needs to keep him feeling secure and safe. He can write the names of those people who care for him and keep him physically and emotionally safe on the roots. Encourage him to think about what qualities he has of his own that keep him 'rooted' and strong. This could be persistence, intelligence, sporting prowess or his sense of humour, for example.

Next move up to the trunk, which is the strongest part of the tree, then ask him to write his strengths and parts of him that the world sees on the trunk. This represents the parts of the self that others have most contact with, just like a tree trunk.

Finally come up to the leaves and branches of the tree. These are perhaps the prettiest and most engaging parts of the tree, especially when swaying in the breeze or laden with blossom in the spring. When the seasons change, the leaves may die off, but they will always grow again the following year. Sometimes the wind blows strongly and the branches get shaken. Ask the child to think about what it means when his 'leaves and branches' are sometimes shaken

– what might stop him from growing healthily sometimes? Write these things or people on the leaves and branches of the tree.

Aims

- To identify risk and resilience factors and to problem-solve around this.

- To increase a sense of self-efficacy.

- To initiate conversations around resilience and stress, which will enable you to assess strengths and vulnerability factors in the child.

Handy hints

Remember that in simple terms, the roots represent the child's resilient qualities and factors in his life that minimise risk. The trunk symbolises the child's strengths and positive aspects of his life. The leaves and branches represent any risk factors or vulnerabilities.

You will need to think with the child or young person about how to maximise their strengths and resilience and how to minimise the risk factors or stressors in their lives. This works particularly well with risk-taking young people.

Self-esteem Time Line

Materials

A large sheet of drawing paper or a roll of wallpaper/lining paper and felt tip pens.

Process

Where children have already experienced abuse, it is important to acknowledge that these experiences should not define them – this child might also be a skilful artist, a strong swimmer, or perhaps really helpful to the teacher in class. Like anybody else, they have had good and bad experiences in their lives. This activity is aimed at building self-esteem by encouraging the child to remember the more positive experiences or relationships they have enjoyed.

Work with the child to create a time line of his life. This can be a simple straight line or might incorporate various twists and turns. Make sure there is room on the paper to add hopes for the future; this is where lining paper can be useful. Focus on:

- The child's positive experiences or memories. This might include celebrations, birthdays, holidays, special friendships, pets, learning to swim, etc.

- Any other events that are important. This could be the birth of siblings, house moves, starting school, etc.

- Hopes and wishes for the future. How does he imagine the future will look? What will he be doing? Where will he live? Who will be with him? How will he feel?

With some children it might be possible later to integrate some of the more difficult or negative memories or experiences into this, while reassuring them they are safe now. When children begin to process these difficult memories they no longer carry such emotional weight, but they must have the right support network around them in order to feel safe enough to this.

Aims

- To put difficult life experiences into perspective. For example, if a child has experienced abuse, this is not the only identity he has.

- To increase the child's ability to have hope for the future and to celebrate successes.

- To increase the child's capacity to separate himself from his abuse or from his abuser(s).

Handy hints

Avoid this activity until you have a sense that the child is now absolutely in a safe place. Where children are still caught up in the emotional experience of their abuse or have not yet learned to feel safe, it can be very difficult for them to focus on the future – the activities in Chapter 3 will help with this.

Some children might find talking about past abuse brings up very strong feelings or memories that are difficult to manage; this might include feeling as if the abuse experience is happening again in the present. You will need to talk to the child about what he needs from you to remain safe in the here and now. Consider anchoring the child to a sense of safety using the *My Safe Place* activity (see page 77), or his parent/carer (if you have them in the room) could provide reassurance or hold him.

Sometimes children and young people can get lost in this activity when looking to the future. It is important to try to guide them towards fairly realistic goals.

Chapter 2

Emotional Literacy and the Body's Emotional Communication

Introduction

We are becoming increasingly aware that 'our bodies generally know what's good for them. Taking notice of feelings of discomfort (for example when we know we've had enough to eat, or when we are tired or in pain) and taking the appropriate action, will result in healthier lifestyles' (Gordon 1995, p.26). Sometimes, however, we get so used to the feelings that we become de-sensitised and disregard our body's communication. We ignore the signals. The same might be said for the body's emotional communication; when we pay attention to the early signals in our bodies that all is not as it should be, we can often avoid more serious or dangerous situations.

Children who have experienced trauma and abuse can become very skilled at avoiding difficult feelings or may have difficulty knowing and expressing directly what they feel or need at a given time. They might have been told their feelings are not valid: as a defensive strategy, they may then learn to minimise, deny, avoid or dissociate. This is a way of numbing and separating from emotions that are too painful or overwhelming to experience. Although it can be an essential survival strategy at the time of the traumatic experience, the separation of body and mind in the longer term can lead to children becoming so detached or cut off from their internal world that they struggle to connect with their own thoughts and feelings. Grotsky *et al.* (2000, p.101) also comment on how 'unexpressed emotions in children also surface as somatic symptoms such as stomach aches, headaches, panic attacks, and bed-wetting'. We need to work towards supporting these children to separate from their abuse history rather than from themselves, to allow them to work towards using the valuable information being communicated by their bodies that might protect them now and in the future. For example, if a child does not allow himself to feel afraid, how will he know to fight or to run from a dangerous situation?

Although children are undoubtedly remarkably resilient at times, we know that traumatic early experiences impact a child's developing capacity to name and regulate emotions. Sunderland explains in simple terms how much influence caregivers have on the development of a child's emotional brain during critical periods of brain growth in the first five years of life:

> With emotionally responsive parenting, vital connections will form in his brain, enabling him to cope well with stresses in later life; be kind and compassionate; have the will and motivation to follow his ambitions and dreams; experience the deepest calm; and be able to love intimately and in peace. (Sunderland 2006, p.22)

Traumatic experiences can also compromise normal developmental processes if the child has neither the skills nor opportunities to express his feelings about them. The ways in which this will impact the child will differ between individuals, but are also dependent on the age and developmental stage of the child. For example, toddlers and pre-school-aged children are generally focusing their energies on the important developmental tasks of gaining control over their basic physical needs (independent feeding or toileting) and their impulses. They are beginning to learn self-control.

Primary school-aged children (aged 4–11) face much more complex social demands: managing peer relationships and the unfamiliar authority of teaching staff as well as processing new academic information every day. It can be hard for these children to learn to function more independently if they are without a secure base. When abuse is ongoing, the child might become more isolated from peers, which also impacts his social development. He may become overwhelmed by strong feelings but lack the skills to express them positively.

A normal adolescent process is to separate from parents/carers; the young person begins to form his identity, but this is much harder to achieve where there is a lack of age and role distinctions in family relationships. Both adolescent girls and boys in abusive situations may also feel further compromised by their increased physiological capacity for sexual response.

Many children who have experienced relational trauma haven't been afforded opportunities to develop basic self-awareness. Bomber describes how 'they are unconscious of their sensations, states and feelings and often can't locate an accurate sense of themselves...will not have had anyone to give them the words to help them describe their sensations, states and feelings in such a way as to make sense of what is going on within their bodies' (2011, pp.111–112). Without support and guidance from a trusted adult to help to manage painful feelings such as loss, frustration or disappointment, children experience prolonged periods with high levels of toxic stress chemicals in their brains and bodies. If a child doesn't have the words to express these emotions, he is likely to express them through behaviour such as a tantrum, aggression or sleeplessness. When a parent/carer consistently and predictably *helps* the child to manage his strong feelings rather than *punishing* the unwanted behaviour, he 'can help their higher brain to develop the nerve pathways essential for naturally regulating such feelings' (Sunderland 2006, p.119).

The starting point in any work around keeping safe has to be to support children towards better self-awareness and then towards learning the skills required to manage strong emotions and to self-soothe. These skills are best assimilated alongside another person, one who is able to model how to find and maintain a state of calm. This process usually begins in infancy, when the baby learns that his distress or arousal will not be experienced as overwhelming as his parent/carer will be there to re-establish equilibrium. Vulnerable children who have not benefited from this experience or who have had inconsistent experiences of co-regulation are therefore at increased risk of becoming dysregulated at times of stress or difficulty.

They have seemingly over-the-top responses to low-level stressors, and can therefore present with behaviours driven by fear and panic. Bomber (2011, p.185) suggests a number of possible influencing factors that include:

- a misinterpretation of the drives and intentions of others
- over-sensitive alarm systems in the child's body, leading to over-reactive behaviour
- struggling to interpret and understand situations they face
- lacking the necessary skills to manage their feelings and behaviour in pro-social or healthy ways
- an inability to respond assertively when required.

In your sessions with children and young people, you must work hard to keep stress to a minimum, while at the same time supporting the child to develop a healthier stress response and a more robust emotional vocabulary. Sometimes adults inadvertently discourage children, not only from having feelings, but also at times from actually experiencing them. For example, a toddler will stumble and fall and his parent/carer may say, 'Don't be a baby. Stop crying. There's nothing to be sad about.' It might be easier for that toddler if his parent/carer said, 'I can see that fall scared you and made you feel really sad.' It is so important that we give children encouragement and permission to talk about their feelings and to create the kind of environment where it feels safe to express rather than repress or deny them. There are various resources you can buy or make yourself to support this, such as paper plate feelings faces, finger puppets or empathy dolls. I also love *The Bear Cards* (Veeken 2012) for younger children, a set of 48 cards with various bear characters showing a wide range of emotions. Although they are expensive, they have multiple applications and provide a safe, fun way to explore and engage in conversations about feelings. Each set also includes a special passkey for free access to a large range of downloads, and there are lots of examples of games to play with the cards.

We cannot underestimate the impact of developmental trauma, and sexual abuse in particular, on the child's body – his sense and understanding of the value, function and danger inherent in the body will shift and change. Memories will be stored in the body, both in unconscious, sensory fragments as well as verbal cognitions for some. It is important in this work to support the connection between the mind and the body for the child in psycho-educative terms. In this chapter you will find activities to support you with this, that also connect with the protective behaviours concept of early warning signs.

Identifying Early Warning Signs

Materials

A large sheet of drawing paper or lining paper that is big enough for the child to lie on, and felt tip pens. You might also consider preparing templates of boy/girl body outlines, if more appropriate.

Process

Either draw around the child so that you have an outline of his body on the paper, draw a freehand body outline or have a template prepared. Explain that when someone is in a potentially dangerous situation, the body gets ready for action – we all experience real, physical feelings in different parts of our bodies that give us a clue this is happening and that we might not be safe. The protective behaviours model would call these early warning signs (or EWS). These tell us we may be at risk of harm, and we need to listen to our bodies so we can make choices to keep us safe. It may be a signal to ask for help if we can't sort the problem out on our own.

Fear affects different people in different ways. Our bodies tell us when our 'normal' sense of safety is being threatened in some way. Be clear that this is a natural response – a physiological process that affects babies from birth, and animals! You can use animal analogies if this might connect with the child, perhaps looking at YouTube videos together to demonstrate the responses of animals in the wild to perceived danger or threat.

Ask the child to think of times when he has felt tense or afraid, even if he hasn't understood why at the time. Remember that once a child becomes aware of his early warning signs, it will be easier to notice how they occur in lots of everyday situations. As well as times of uncertainty or overt danger, you can also use examples of times when it might be *fun or exciting to feel a little bit scared*, such as learning to roller blade or skateboard, sledging down a massive hill or watching a scary film. This could also include occasions when the child is doing something new for the first time, as it's a normal part of growing up to have these adventures. The thing about adventures, though, is that they are usually something we *choose* to do, and we can stop if we decide we want to. If we don't like the experience, we don't have to do it again. It always makes sense when we get an early warning sign to stop, take a deep breath, and think of the possible consequences before we take a sensible or measured risk.

There might be other times when the child feels *afraid but still in control*. He might be scared about going to the dentist for a filling or taking a spelling test, but with preparation and support, some of the anxiety can be alleviated. 'This ability to face and take control of reasonable fears is an important skill to enhance' (Gordon 1995, pp.32–33), so it is vital that we offer children encouragement and support to deal with the challenges they face in daily life. The activities in Chapter 5 will help with this too.

The third possible scenario is when *the fear feels out of control – or a personal emergency*. In these circumstances, children need to know that all social norms and niceties are less important than being safe. They may need to do things that they would never think of doing in normal circumstances. Emergencies can, of course, come in all shapes and sizes, ranging from feeling sick on a car journey to someone trying to abduct a child from the park. The child needs to know that it is vital to listen to his internal body messages at these times, and not to worry about what anyone else might say or do or think of him. If children practise tuning into their early warning signs in everyday, non-emergency situations, it means they are more likely to be internalised to become an automatic response in real, potentially life-threatening emergencies (Gordon 1995).

After exploring these different scenarios, identify the signs and signals (or early warning signs) the child's body gives him at these times, and draw or write them on the body outline. You might need to offer prompts or share some of your own experiences – I often use the example of a near miss while driving my car. Early warning signs might include sweating palms, blushing, shaking, breathing heavily, wanting to run away, heart rate increasing, stammering, throat tightening, headache, biting lips, butterflies in the tummy or clenching fists.

It is also important to go on to think about what to do if the child notices his early warning signs, and how best to assess all the available options. Running might be an option if the child is a faster runner than the person causing the emergency, or if there is someone or somewhere safe to run to. Screaming or yelling are also good options to let people around you know there is an emergency, but only if you are near someone who would hear you and not out on a remote, country lane. Ultimately the success of any strategy is dependent on the power differential between the child and potential source of danger. Sometimes the child is simply not in a position to take effective action and that will never be his fault; sometimes he will need a safe adult to help him regain a sense of safety. Sometimes the groomer's tactics are so effective that the child doesn't get an early warning sign.

I find it helpful to connect this activity with thinking around safety planning or safety networks (see *Establishing Personal Networks* on page 64 and the *Child Safety Plan* on page 119). It is important to stress that this is a time to tell and not be worried about getting told off for telling tales or trying to get someone else in trouble.

Aims

- To educate the child about the impact of stress and fear on the body.

- To help the child recognise his own early warning signs.

- To normalise the child's physiological responses and feelings in relation to danger or a lack of felt safety.

- To increase the child's sense of control at times when he is feeling unsafe.

- To connect with the idea of building a safety network and asking for help when necessary.

Handy hints

It may not be appropriate to draw around the child if he has been sexually abused or is uncomfortable with such close physical proximity to you. You may be better advised to draw a generic outline of a body or ask the child to draw one and use this in the same way.

Some children may find the concept of early warning signs difficult to connect with in terms of their own experience. Children who have experienced trauma and abuse may have learned to ignore these signs – they become so accustomed to feeling unsafe that it feels 'normal' and they pay their early warning signs no attention. Martin (2007, p.9) suggests helping a child track and observe their bodily responses to minor stressors through simple activities such as popping a balloon, watching a jack-in-the-box pop up, balancing on a beam or wearing a blindfold to cross the room. I think for some children this might be easier to manage with a parent/carer alongside them, and for others what seem to be innocuous stressors might be trauma triggers, so be mindful of this if you plan to go down this route.

You might also think with the child about how his body feels when fear or tension is not around. How might life be different if fear and tension visited less often? What are the things he would like to do more of? Some children can find dealing with abstract concepts like this difficult; you might want to try scaling techniques with these children. For example, on a scale of 1:10 where 1 means totally relaxed and not at all scared and 10 means the most terrified you have ever been in your life, where would you place yourself on the scale? You could offer different scenarios as a comparison, for example, where are you now? Where would you be if you were lost in the city centre? Where are you when you are in your bed at night?

There are also lots of stories that can help with exploring early warning signs. *Little Red Riding Hood* is a classic, but I also like *The Owl Who Was Afraid of the Dark* (Tomlinson 2008), and in early years, perhaps *We're Going on a Bear Hunt* (Rosen 1989).

With some children, you will need to explore the difference between getting an early warning sign and telling a trusted adult, and tale telling when you don't have an early warning sign. Check out whether the child should tell with some hypothetical scenarios, for example:

Would you tell an adult:

> If someone dropped his pencil on the floor?
>
> If someone kicked your friend on purpose?
>
> If someone didn't eat his lunch at school and threw it in the bin?
>
> If someone drew on the wall?
>
> If someone accidentally pushed you over in the playground playing tag?
>
> If an adult you didn't know asked you to keep a secret?

Playing Feelings Detective

Materials

Paper or prepared body outline (girl or boy/adolescent) and felt tip pens. Feelings cards are optional, as are detective dress-up props – cue the Sherlock Holmes hat and magnifying glass, if you are that way inclined!

Process

For children who have experienced trauma and neglect, there can be a disconnect between the sensations experienced in their bodies and their emotional worlds. However, they can potentially learn a lot by gaining a better understanding of these connections.

> When children understand that the body sensation may be signalling an emotional feeling, they learn to pay attention to the emotional feeling. When they know what the emotional feeling is, they can search back to why they are having it. They can determine if there is something they can do to change what occurs to make them feel this way… Breaking the chain between a body sensation and action is very important for children. (Cavanagh Johnson 1998a, p.135)

So in this activity talk to the child about building a personal body map of sensations to help him understand his feelings better. The child will be a *body detective*. You could provide some feelings cards as a prompt (see below), or ask the child to suggest strong feelings he experiences most regularly. It's always good to leave a few blank ones for feelings you might not anticipate.

Happy	Excited	Ashamed
Sad	Tearful	Worried
Scared	Anxious	Lonely
Loved	Angry	Stressed
Confused	Irritated	Jealous

You can either offer an appropriate body outline to the child, or assess whether it might be safe to draw around the child's own body. Starting with the strongest feeling, ask the child to imagine a scenario where he would experience this feeling, and then locate where in his body he feels the emotion. Then annotate the diagram with the name of the feeling and different situations where it might be experienced.

Talk about how helpful it can be to understand how the physical sensation we have in our body connects with an emotion, as this can then help us make better decisions about how to act or respond in a given situation. Often all that children experience is the sometimes overwhelming bodily sensation without connecting it to an emotion; this can lead to action without thinking it through, and choices that are not always safe.

Aims

- To increase the child's ability to tune into ways in which feelings are held in his body and where they are located.

- To learn which feelings are easier for him to locate or name than others.

- To learn whether a particular feeling state dominates or is denied.

Handy hints

For younger children, an alternative might be to give the child a selection of different coloured crayons and ask him to create a key, matching colours to a range of feelings: happy, sad, excited, scared, anxious, angry, calm, ashamed, jealous. For each feeling, ask the child to colour where in his body he feels it most. For example:

Blue	→	Sad
Black	→	Scared
Brown	→	Ashamed
Red	→	Angry
Green	→	Jealous
Orange	→	Anxious
Yellow	→	Happy

Notice whether it has been an easy or difficult task for him. Talk about whether certain feelings dominate in particular parts of his body, and see if you can encourage him to talk about times when he has felt scared, happy, sad, etc. Stress the idea that when feelings are kept hidden inside for too long they can lead to aches and pains, particularly for those children with frequent tummy aches or headaches.

My House or My Castle

Materials

A doll's house with furniture and dolls, or a castle with soldiers. If this isn't possible, you can use template outlines of a house or castle, preferably enlarged to A3 size; you will also need felt tip pens.

Process

This is an adaptation of an exercise developed by the NSPCC (1997, pp.16–17). Depending on the child's interests and personality, use either a house or a castle. Talk to the child about the house/castle, directing him to the front door/drawbridge on which you have written: 'Please knock and wait.' Explore with the child who might live there. Is it his home? If not, who might we find if we go inside? Where might the people be in the house/castle, and what are they doing? How does he feel about the people or the rooms he describes?

You can expand this to think about which areas of the home/castle are private and who might be allowed in. You could link this with the activity on page 100, *Private versus Public Spaces and Places*. Is there anywhere in the home/castle that doesn't feel safe or comfortable? This is potentially a helpful approach to use with children living in a residential setting – either in a mainstream children's home or with children with additional needs who may access short breaks. It can help you to explore routines in the home and who does what. Where does the child spend most of his time and with whom, doing what?

Aims

- To explore the child's everyday experiences.

- To explore family relationships with a particular focus on safety and on how emotions are expressed.

- To assess the child's understanding of personal space and privacy.

- To connect feelings with people or places in the child's life.

Handy hints

If there is a likelihood that the child has been abused in the family home or placement, you will need to approach this with caution. If you are using the activity as part of an investigative process, be mindful to avoid leading questions that could compromise any criminal investigation that may follow.

If using templates, you could expand this activity to support further exploration of feelings towards other family members, by asking the child to draw them in the house/castle doing what they would do on a typical day. You could suggest adding thought or speech bubbles to help you understand what people are thinking or feeling. You may need to prompt with questions that will increase understanding, for example: 'I wonder if that's your mummy? What is she thinking right now?' Try to explore different areas of family life and times of the day, as well as what makes people happy, sad, angry, etc. You could have some feelings faces to use to help the child attach a feeling to a room or a person.

The castle technique has the advantage of being able to bring a dungeon into the scenario, in which children can potentially choose to place their abusers. They could have guards to protect the castle walls from unsafe people or have a moat filled with sharks or crocodiles to keep unsafe people out. Ask the child when he would choose to raise the drawbridge and to whom he would deny entry. Might the excluded people be able to do anything now or in the future that would make them safe enough to allow into the castle or out of the dungeon?

Feelings Charades

Materials

A series of cards depicting different feeling states such as angry, sad, afraid, anxious or excited. You can prepare these beforehand or make them together during the session. They can be either written or drawn as feelings faces.

Process

This is a great activity to do with family or sibling groups or if you have the parent/carer in the session with the child. It is great for assessing whether a child can recognise facial expressions and can connect emotions with situational events. There are a number of different permutations:

- Basic: The parent/carer or worker takes a card and acts out the feeling state. The child must guess the feeling. You can then reverse this so that the child takes a turn acting out the feeling while the parent/carer/worker guesses.

- Reverse: The parent/carer or worker acts out what the child looks like during a particular feeling state and the child must guess the feeling. Then switch roles.

- Trigger situations: The parent/carer or worker acts out a difficult situation and the child has to identify possible emotional responses. You can use the feeling cards to help with identification. Reverse roles if appropriate. In this situation you might include different scenarios relating to keeping safe, for example, being asked to keep a secret from a parent/carer, being asked to meet someone the child has met online, etc.

Alternatively, the child and parent/carer or worker choose a feeling card together and then take turns to act out a scenario that might evoke that feeling, with the worker or parent/carer guessing the emotion.

Aims

- To have some fun with the child.

- To build on the parent/carer–child relationship, with the worker as facilitator.

- To learn more about the ways in which the child communicates his feelings. If you can learn more about how to read a child's cues and patterns of relating, you will be better able to respond to changes in his feeling state in the sessions.

- To assess whether the child can link feelings with events and behaviours.

Handy hints

There are infinite variations on this game, so feel free to adapt to fit the situation, as this activity could be done with individual children, sibling groups or with a child and parent/carer. I have adapted the activity from Blaustein and Kinniburgh (2010) who use it when working with a child's caregiving system to help parents/carers learn to accurately and empathically understand and respond to the child's actions, communications, needs and feelings (Blaustein and Kinniburgh 2010, pp.65–73). They talk about becoming feelings detectives (also see *Playing Feelings Detective* on page 48), noticing in the child how he communicates different feelings in order to better respond to the emotion that underlies the behaviour. Communication cues include the child's facial expression, tone of voice, how much or how little he verbalises speech, his posture and non-verbal communication.

Golding and Todd (1994, pp.18–19) suggest miming a character to develop vocabulary relating to feelings, and to allow practice of non-verbal communication. Ask the child to improvise a movement that depicts a number of different scenarios, such as:

- an angry frog

- a toddler who is scared of the dark

- a bad tempered prince

- a frantic parent looking for a lost child

- a proud pop star at the end of a concert.

At the end of the mimes you can talk about how the feelings were demonstrated. Discuss the importance of posture, facial expression and general body awareness to depict the scene well.

Feelings Rocket

Materials
Paper and felt tip pens or collage materials to make a 3D rocket – card and Sellotape™ (or Scotch Tape) or a used kitchen towel roll.

Process
This activity is for those children who fear that expressing strong, 'big' feelings might be overwhelming for themselves, their parents/carers, or even for workers. It is an acknowledgment that some feelings are tricky to manage. We might not want to feel so much of them. We might sometimes not want to think about them at all. Alternatively, sometimes we might want to share the load with someone, preferably

someone on the child's safety network (see *Establishing Personal Networks* on page 64).

First, make the rocket – most children would enjoy making it with you, but you might decide to have 'one you prepared earlier', if time is tight. Take your tube or roll your card into a tube and secure with Sellotape™. Make a triangular piece of card into a cone shape to sit on top of the tube/rocket. Don't secure this initially as you need to be able to remove it to add the feelings. You can add rocket wings if you are feeling especially creative.

Introduce the rocket to the child as a 'feelings rocket'. The child can use the rocket to send any feelings he'd like to get rid of up, into outer space. He could make some mini feelings faces to put in the rocket, write the feeling on some paper, or represent the feelings symbolically with a colour or shape.

You may be able to extend the activity to talk about how normal it is to have a range of feelings – both positive and negative – and that it can help to talk about them. You could examine the feelings in the rocket individually, and think about times the child has felt that way recently – what was the context, how did he manage the feeling, who could he go to for support with the feeling?

Aims

- To normalise strong or difficult feelings.

- To allow the child to externalise strong or difficult feelings.

- To begin to problem-solve around strong feelings and build supportive networks for the child.

Handy hints

This can be done on an individual basis or with a family group, where siblings can take turns to add a difficult feeling into the rocket. Some may choose to put the feelings in anonymously if they are hard to acknowledge publically. This is a good activity for children aged between 6 and 12 or older if they have a learning disability or developmental delay. Younger children may struggle to conceptualise feelings identification in this sense.

You can choose to send the rocket off to space forever, or sometimes children choose to re-visit the feelings in the rocket in subsequent sessions. This can be a useful tool for helping children realise that feelings are not static – they do change in intensity and frequency over time.

A variation on this to convey safety, permission and control is the 'Feelings Train' described by the NSPCC (1997, pp.33–35). This can be used with children from the age of four upwards, and all you need are three basic steam train templates. In the first train feelings letters/ faces are bubbling and trapped in the boiler and the driver looks unhappy. Talk to the child about how the driver might feel and what might happen to the engine if the feelings can't get out.

In the next image the feelings letters or faces are exploding out of the boiler and the driver looks upset. How might the driver feel about this? Does the child ever feel like this? What happens? Normalise these feelings – we all have upset or angry feelings that sometimes spill out of us. There are things we can do to stop them exploding all of the time and to feel more in control.

In the third image, the feelings letters or faces are coming safely out of the boiler with the driver in charge of the lever. Ask the child how the driver is feeling and what is happening now in the image. Explain that the lever means that the feelings can be let out when the driver chooses. He is in charge and he lets the feelings out when he feels it safe to do so. Talk about what might make this possible for the child.

Weather Report

Materials

A comfortable chair in which to sit, paper and drawing materials.

Process

Ask the child to sit up straight in a chair with both feet on the floor, and to relax his neck and shoulders as much as possible. If it feels safe to do so, he can close his eyes, and should breathe calmly and slowly.

Explain how hard it can be to express how our body is feeling, though it feels so many different things. Ask how he feels in the here and now. Does his body feel relaxed? How is his heart beat? Ask him to pay attention to his chest and stomach area next. How is it feeling? Can he look inside and sense his 'internal weather'? When you feel good, your internal weather might be sunny and bright, with not a cloud in the sky. When you are feeling angry, you might feel a storm is brewing or there is a thunderstorm inside. If you are feeling sad or lonely, you might say the weather is rainy or freezing cold. Ask these questions:

- Is it stormy?

- Is it windy?

- Is it sunny?

- Is it foggy?

- Is it calm?

- Is it icy cold?

Is there a combination of different kinds of weather to report? Is it cloudy, with a hint of sunshine peeking through? Is it brisk and breezy? Is there a chance his internal weather might change, just as the weather outside often changes? The sunshine might be hidden by clouds or a rainy day might be lit by a rainbow when the sun comes out.

Imagine what the weather might look like – it might be a colour, a view or an image. You then have the option of moving on to depict an image of the weather inside on paper – sometimes young people find it liberating to use their non-dominant hand to draw with, especially if they're unsure about their artistic abilities.

Aims

- To make connections between felt sensations in the body with emotions, and to externalise these.

- To notice where in the body these senses are held, and to create a dialogue between body and mind.

Handy hints

This activity is best used with older children. When the young person has finished creating the image, check in with how he is feeling right at that moment. Is it different to the picture he has created? If it does seem different, it is fine to add to or change the image. This reinforces the idea that feelings can shift and change in moments of time.

Sense Memory

Materials

None – just some ideas of different sensory experiences and a room that's big enough to move around in and mime.

Process

This is taken from Golding and Todd (1994, p.19), who use drama techniques in schools to teach protective behaviours. Ask the child to mime a series of different actions as you give a verbal description. The emphasis should be on reflecting the sensory experience. Here are some examples, but use your imagination to create others:

- Walk barefoot on hot sand, come to a freezing cold pool of water, step carefully at first, then experience the sense of relief as the icy water cools your toes.

- Pick up a ripe orange, feel its bumpy texture, peel it carefully with a knife or your fingers, take a segment and taste it. It's the sweetest orange you have ever tasted! You might then feel the sticky juice on your fingers.

- Pick up your mobile phone, dial a number and listen to it ring out. No one answers, so end the call with some disappointment.

- Pick up a heavy suitcase and carry it as carefully as you can to the other side of the room and place it down gently. Open the zip and take something really precious and delicate from inside, but try not to let anyone see what it is.

- You're in a flower garden, listen to the buzzing bees and approach the most beautiful flower you can see in the garden. You may need to look hard to find the right one. Then lean in and smell the delightful scent of the flower in bloom.

- Someone has given you a beautifully wrapped gift in a big box. Carefully unwrap the silky ribbon and remove the wrapping paper. Can you hear the crinkly sound of the paper? Open the flaps carefully and look inside – what can you see? What a wonderful surprise!

Aims

- To support the child to explore feelings and different experiences.

- To support the child to connect with his sensory experiences.

- To enhance the child's listening skills and his capacity to follow instructions.

- To have some fun.

Handy hints

This is a great activity for kinaesthetic learners or for children who respond better to active methods; if the child is restless or overactive in your session, it's always worth trying to get him moving proactively rather than trying to make him sit still. Do these mimes together; it's really good fun and can help overcome self-consciousness or embarrassment.

Chapter 3

Feeling Safe and Understanding What it Means

Introduction

Feeling safe and understanding what it means is the first theme of the protective behaviours model and really needs some unpicking with vulnerable children. You cannot assume they know what 'safe' feels or looks like. You cannot assume they know they have the right to feel safe all the time, because in reality, they may not ever feel truly safe, either physically or psychologically. They may not have experienced safety both in terms of their body and their brain as well as their environment. So in this phase of the work you will be exploring feeling safe and helping children learn to experience, understand and eventually enjoy 'felt' safety.

A vital component of this work is supporting the child or young person to understand the body's physiological danger response. This means sharing information around the body's alarm system and trauma responses where appropriate. The main teaching points are as follows:

- The body's alarm system: All mammals have alarm systems that are designed to protect them from danger. In the past they developed to protect humans from predators. Now they also register alarm when humans experience psychological stress. This helps our bodies prepare to deal with danger when it arrives.

- The human danger response: When the brain recognises danger is close, it gets our body ready to deal with it. We then have three options – fight it, get away from it (flight), or freeze. What option we choose depends on the situation we find ourselves in. If you are bigger and stronger than the threat, you might decide to fight. If you were crossing the road and a car came racing towards you, you would probably try to run, because you couldn't fight it, and if you froze and stood still, you'd get hit. If you saw a grizzly bear you might freeze because you'd have no chance of fighting it, and you might not be fast enough to run away.

- Our body gives us the energy we need to survive: We need a lot of energy to fight, run or freeze. When our brain recognises danger is close, the action part of the brain sends a signal to our body to release chemicals – just like putting petrol in a car. Older children may be interested to hear more detail about how the brain responds at these times. In this case, explain that one of the most important alarm systems in the brain is called the 'amygdala'. One of its main jobs is to work out the emotional meaning of everything that happens to us. If the amygdala senses that something might be a threat, it talks to another part of the brain called the hypothalamus. This part of the brain releases the stress hormones that prepare the body for action, with attention now all on the threat.

Blaustein and Kinniburgh (2010, pp.277–278) suggest playing a 'Fight, Flight or Freeze' game. They look at a range of different scenarios and ask the child to decide whether the person in the scenario is in fight, flight or freeze mode. For example, a cat is crossing the road when a car starts towards it. The cat just stands there (freezes). You could also relate the same theory to scenarios you know the child has experienced. For example, when another pupil teased him at school, he hit him in the nose (fight). When he was delivering a newspaper on his paper round, a dog raced out of the back garden towards him. He turned and ran out of the garden as fast as he could (flight).

You will need to support the child to connect with his own bodily sensations and with his sensory experience (the activities in Chapter 2 will also help you with this). Relate this to 'false alarms', where he might hear or see something that reminds him of a traumatic or threatening event. Explain that his brain has learned to recognise those reminders because in the past, it meant something dangerous was about to happen. If a child lived with lots of shouting and violence, a loud noise or a yell (even in excitement) could activate his brain's alarm system. If he was often left at home alone, feeling lonely or hearing the front door close (even if there was someone else in the house), this might turn on his alarm. It's really important to support children to notice their false alarms; if we can learn the triggers and how the child typically responds when his body is flooded with stress hormones, then we can help him find ways to engage his thinking brain to work out whether the danger is real.

Sometimes children are able to talk about what the word 'safety' means for them: they can clearly articulate *when* they experience safety, *where* they experience safety and *with whom*. For others it is much more difficult to connect with, but you don't have to over-complicate it. One of the most powerful sessions I remember was with a girl and her foster carer; we suspected the girl had experienced sexual harm, but she had never made a disclosure. When my plan A for that particular session failed to engage her, I simply wrote SAFE in bubble writing. As she coloured in the word, we began to talk about what safety meant for her, and she began to draw images to record our discussion. This included basic, practical safety measures such as having window locks and securing the doors at night to keep intruders out, as well as having fire blankets in the kitchen, carbon monoxide and smoke alarms. However, it then also extended to include the domestic violence she had witnessed, and the right for all children to be protected from physical and emotional harm. This, in turn, developed into a discussion about other ways touch could hurt, and she let us know for the first time that a family friend had sexually abused her. In the many sessions that followed, she chose not to talk about this again with me, but knowing her foster carer now understood what she had experienced seemed to lift a huge weight from her shoulders and she was able to move forward. Sometimes the simplest ideas prove to be the most effective ones in supporting vulnerable children and young people.

Acrostic poems can also be successful in exploring what being safe means to the child, as can encouraging him to make a safety poster displaying the theme. For children who need more active methods of engagement, Lippett suggests writing small messages around rights and responsibilities, for example, 'We all have the right to feel safe', and then placing them inside balloons and releasing them outdoors (1990, p.11).

You also need to think about times when it's okay to feel a little bit scared or unsafe and normalise this for the child too. Talk about activities that might be scary but still good fun, like going really high on a climbing wall or learning to ride a bike. Excitement and adventure should be fun, but of course what is fun for one child may be too scary for another; rides at a theme park are great for observing this in action. Adult-led risk-taking can be a great boost to resilience and confidence. Trying something new for the first time and asking for help to succeed is really important, as is developing the capacity to say 'no' without feeling pressure from other people (see *Alternative Simon Says* on page 116 and *Identifying Early Warning Signs* on page 44).

In this regard, it's also important to understand why children often don't tell when they're unsafe or when they experience abuse. There are many complex reasons for this, including the fact they may not recognise the abuse as abuse, and may therefore not feel unsafe or have any early warning signs. Other explanations may include:

- embarrassment and shame
- not knowing it was wrong
- fear because they've been threatened by the abuser
- not wanting to get into trouble
- thinking nobody will believe them
- not having the words to say
- liking or loving the abuser and wanting to protect the abuser, especially where it is a close relative or parent
- thinking other people already know about it.

It can sometimes be easier for children to talk to someone outside the family first – perhaps because they want to protect their parent/carer. This is why establishing a network of supportive adults around children is so important. It's the telling that's the bravest, most important thing for children rather than whom they choose to tell. Remember that people who abuse children rely on secrecy. They try to silence the child and build trust with adults, counting on the adults to be silent too if they have a worry about the child. So the first step to tackling this secrecy is to support children to develop open and trusting relationships with the people in their safety network, and to help them recognise when their sense of safety has been breached.

In this chapter you will find activities that will help children and young people connect with a feeling of safety and relaxation in their bodies (see *Relaxation Techniques* on page 80 and *My Safe Place* on page 77), as well as looking at practical strategies to build safety such as identifying safe adults (*Establishing Personal Networks* on page 64) and *Safety Rules* (see page 67).

Establishing Personal Networks

Materials
Paper, pens (sequins, stickers or other collage materials are optional for decoration). You might want to bring a prepared template of a hand, ladder, flower or umbrella.

Process
This activity connects with the protective behaviours theme, that 'there is nothing so awful we cannot talk to someone about it'. This has been extended in recent years to include 'there is also nothing so small that we cannot share it'. We all need a personal network, a group of people in our lives who are there to celebrate with us when times are good and to support us when we need them, for whatever reason. The protective behaviours model also suggests that children should persist in seeking help until they feel certain that someone has listened, understood and helped them to feel safe again. It is important in this activity to stress that if the first person the child asks doesn't help (they may not believe him or they may be busy dealing

with another problem), he must try someone else in his network. The child will only know his problem has been dealt with when he feels safe again. You might need to role-play some different scenarios with the child practising asking for help and persevering if he doesn't feel heard. It's also worth reiterating that it's okay to break the rules in an emergency to get an adult's attention straight away, for example, by interrupting a conversation, by saying 'no' or by breaking a secret.

There are various options for this activity depending on the age, gender and interests of the child, but the most commonly used is the 'Hand of Safety'. I like to use the child's own hand to draw around, or I might have a generic hand template ready. Other ideas are to use a flower with five or six petals, or an umbrella or ladder with a similar number of different sections. Tell the child that you would like to learn about the safe people in his life, who he would go to if he was worried, scared or had a problem. Ask the child to try to identify five safe people and write their names on the individual fingers of the hand (or petals, spokes or rungs, depending on what image you are using). You will be reinforcing the importance of these people throughout the session, so you could encourage the child to decorate the hand to reflect its importance, or represent the accessibility of the person with the length of finger. Martin suggests the criteria for being a network person is an adult who will listen, believe, be available and accessible, and who will take action if required to protect the child and help him feel safe once more. Although it is not necessary to be this prescriptive, she develops the idea further, and suggests:

> using the thumb for an adult that lives in your home, second and third fingers for school staff and the fourth and fifth fingers for family or community members not living in the same home, for example another parent (if not living in the home), grandparent, neighbour, aunts or uncles or adults at out of school activities (e.g. sport coach, scout leader), parents of friends, church leaders, family doctor, etc. (Martin 2007, p.13)

You can then talk about what it is about each person that makes the child feel safe or whether he would go to different people for different problems. Think about whom the child will be able to talk to about difficult feelings the work might engender in between sessions.

Aims

- To develop the idea of the team or system around the child supporting safety, thereby increasing his feelings of security and broadening his options for seeking help.

- To learn more about the child's view of his network and what 'safety' means to him.

- To help the child identify safe people if he is struggling to do this, and to explore what being a safe person means. How could these people support the child to keep safe?

- To explore the concept of persistence in the pursuit of safety.

Handy hints

Although this is a good activity for younger children, adolescents will also benefit from a conversation about safe people in their lives, as they often take risks and can find it hard to accurately assess whether others are trustworthy.

Children will sometimes only want to include friends, pets or siblings on their 'Hand of Safety'; these are not network people. It is important to check out who the person is before their name goes on the image, particularly given that some children will want to name known perpetrators of abuse, and adolescents will usually want to include their peers. Try to ensure that the child has identified a range of adults in different settings – home, school, short breaks placement, after-school club, etc.

Within my sessions we write letters together to the people in the child's network to encourage them to support the child with keeping safe, and to let them know the child has identified them as in his safety network. This should mean that these individuals will be more likely to respond quickly to the child's requests for help or support which, of course, may not always be explicitly made. Encourage the child to share good news with his network people to open the lines of communication for when they are most needed. You could also rehearse different scenarios where the child might need to contact his network person.

From time to time have a network review as people can come and go from children's lives, and it's important to make sure the child then updates his network as appropriate. For example, he may have a change of social worker or move classes in school at the end of the year. Others on the network may have been tried and found wanting. On a positive note, new people may come into children's lives who would be perfect network members.

Lippett (1990, p.65) talks about using songs with younger children to reinforce learning around protective behaviours, particularly patterning over well-known children's rhymes. For example, in relation to building a safety network, to the tune of 'Old MacDonald' you could sing:

> *Katie Wrench has a network, e-i-e-i-o.*
> *And in that network she has her mum, e-i-e-i-o.*
> *With a talk here, and a talk there.*
> *Here a talk, there a talk, everywhere they talk,*
> *Katie Wrench has a network, e-i-e-i-o!*

Safety Rules

Materials
Paper and felt tip pens and collage materials.

Process
This is adapted from guidance developed by the child protection charity, The Lucy Faithfull Foundation (no date), in their booklet *What's the Problem? A Guide for Parents of Children and Young People Who Have Got into Trouble Online.* Where there are worries in a family about a child or young person's behaviour (e.g. accessing pornography online or truanting from school) or specific vulnerabilities, it can help to come up with shared rules:

- Talk about the warning signs. These will be different for every child in different settings. It could be increased time spent online or out of the family home; it could be a change in mood or attitude.

- Open the lines of communication. Talking about safety shouldn't be a one-off event with any child, but the need for it to be an ongoing process is heightened for vulnerable children. It is important for the adult to set the tone by talking about difficult issues openly such as sex and relationships or drug and alcohol use. Make sure everyone knows it's okay to talk about any worries they may have.

- Set clear boundaries and stick to them. These may be broad or may relate to a very specific concern around an event that has already happened (e.g. sexting, meeting a stranger you have only talked to online). Boundaries will need adjustment, perhaps as the child gets older or as trust develops.

- Seek help and advice if needed. There are various online resources cited throughout this book. However, you may also need to ask for specialist support, for example, from children's social work services, child and adolescent mental health services or a third sector organisation, around risks of child sexual exploitation, for example.

- Identify who everyone involved will talk to if there is a worry or concern about a particular behaviour or person. This might be each other, someone on the child's safety network (see *Establishing Personal Networks* on page 64) or a professional who can offer support.

The plan might then look like this:

Who is involved in the safety rules?

Who are we worried about?

What are we worried might happen?

What will happen if things are going wrong for X?

What might we notice? How might X act? What might X say?

For the child/young person and their parents/carers you can then look at:

Parent/carer	Young person
How does X say he feels?	How do I feel?
What does X do?	How do I act?
How does X act towards others?	How do I try to cover things up if they're going wrong for me?
What does X say?	What am I thinking about?
Anything else I might notice?	Anything else I might notice?

Next look at what steps need to be taken to ensure everyone is safe and who is responsible. For example, the computer may need to be in a public space rather than the young person's bedroom, so his parent/carer might set it up in the dining room. Or the young person's phone may need to be handed in to an adult before bed, so he might be responsible for turning it off and putting it on the kitchen counter by 9pm.

You also need to agree what will happen if someone isn't doing what has been agreed, how long the plan should be in place for, and how often it should be reviewed.

Aims

- To agree shared rules around safety.

- To maintain lines of communication in relation to safety between the adult and child/young person.

- To help young people and their parents/carers work together on making joint decisions.

Handy hints

This is ideally something that should be done collaboratively with the young person, with all family members on board, as a way of keeping everyone safe. It is as much about clarifying what we want young people to do as well as what we don't want them to do. Therefore, you might choose to add in a section to the plan that looks at building resilience and achieving goals. You can look at activities for the young person/family to work towards. For example, a goal might be to spend more time with friends offline. The steps to achieving this might include parents/carers checking out the local rugby team or other out-of-school activities.

Where you need to create more generic safety rules, perhaps with a younger child, you could make a safety poster or poem to develop the child's own safety rules. Encourage the child to think about what sorts of situations might be risky, or how others might persuade him to do things that might be unsafe. Of course there are ambiguities in many different scenarios, and it is important to acknowledge this. Allow the child to come to his own realisations or decisions around safety where you can, so he can take ownership of the rules, although it is always helpful to have some idea of the basic principles you would want to include:

- Never go alone with someone you don't know unless a trusted adult tells you it is okay.

- Be aware of behaviour in others that might be deemed 'suspicious' (refer to *Understanding Emotional Grooming* on page 146 and *Normal or Harmful? Resisting Grooming Tactics* on page 149). You might need to prepare some ideas of suspicious behaviour beforehand to think about together. For example, being offered bribes or favours for no good reason, being asked to go somewhere when no one else is around, someone being too nice or generous, or conversely someone using threatening words, behaviour or body language.

- Pay attention to your body's communication and your felt emotion to give you clues about what is safe or unsafe. (Connect with *Identifying Early Warning Signs* on page 44.)

- If someone wants you to keep a secret that feels bad or unsafe, be suspicious of their motivation. Listen to your 'gut feeling'. (Connect with *Secrets and Secret Enablers* on page 121.)

- Ask for help from someone you trust if you feel unsafe, and be persistent until you get the help you need (see *Establishing Personal Networks* on page 64).

- Identify a family password, and agree that you will only go with someone who knows the family password.

Safety Continuum

Materials

Felt tip pens and a large sheet of paper.

Process

As much as we would like to shield our children from danger and always be there to protect them from harm, it should also be part of growing up to experience adventure and some risk-taking. We will not always physically be there with our children, so working together on a safety continuum supports them in learning how to scale risk-taking behaviour more reliably for themselves. This continuum and activity is adapted from Martin's book, *The Parents Helping Handbook* (2007, pp.7–8).

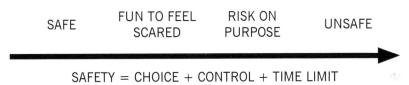

Talk to the child or young person about how you need to have a choice, some kind of control or a time limit on an activity in order to experience a sense of safety. You may need to explore the differences here between emotional, physical and psychological safety using a series of different scenarios. As you draw and work on the safety continuum together, you can include personal experiences or connections for the child across four domains:

- Safe: Safety will look and feel different for every child, and what might start off feeling safe might quickly change into something that feels much riskier. For example, a play fight that begins with tickles and wrestling may begin to feel less safe when the child feels he needs to wee or when one child hurts the other. For older adolescents, kissing and fondling a partner may feel safe to begin with, but if one party begins to put pressure on the other to go further, this may feel unsafe, particularly if the partner is physically stronger.

- Fun to feel scared: This idea fits with the *Identifying Early Warning Signs* activity on page 44, but the key to this area is that of *feeling in control, feeling you have a choice* or that there is *a clear time limit*. You might choose to go on a rollercoaster at the fair, feel terrified during the ride and a little out of control because you can't get off, but you still know the ride will eventually stop. There is a clear time limit – no ride lasts forever. Alternatively, you may drag your sledge through the snow to the top of a steep hill and scream with fear as you ride all the way to the bottom, but you can also choose not to climb the hill again – you are in control of whether you ride again. You may be watching a scary movie or reading a thriller or horror story, but in both these scenarios you will usually have control over whether you watch or read to the end. You typically have a choice in the matter.

- Risk on purpose: Sometimes we have to take a calculated risk to achieve a goal, even if it doesn't feel good or safe in the moment. An example of this might be taking off your arm bands in the swimming pool as you learn to swim, or removing the stabilisers from your first bike. Often these kinds of risks are best taken with a trusted adult alongside, especially when the child may feel out of control, such as at a trip to the dentist or having uncomfortable medical procedures.

- Unsafe: Many of our children will feel disconnected from feelings of danger while others will see danger everywhere; don't make assumptions about what might make them feel threatened, insecure or unprotected. Similarly, don't presume that the child will recognise unsafe behaviour or situations – you may need to offer different scenarios to explore together. For example, children who have experienced low levels of adult supervision may not consciously connect being at home alone or out on the streets in the dark with being unsafe – it may just feel normal.

It will also be important to connect with times where a child may start off feeling unsafe at one end of the continuum and end up feeling safe. This might connect with having a different teaching assistant in school, learning a new skill or visiting a new place for the first time.

Aims

- To explore the concept of self-efficacy and of making good choices.

- To explore the idea of risk-taking in different contexts.

- To connect with work around early warning signs.

- To normalise the range of experiences we all have around safety and to demonstrate the possibility of movement through time and with experience along the safety continuum.

Handy hints

There are some great ideas from the Theraplay world around helping both the child with risk-taking behaviours and the most risk-averse child to face challenges with adult support. This might be as simple as balancing beanbags or cushions on his head or keeping a balloon up in the air and not letting it touch the ground (see Booth and Jernberg 2010).

For adolescents in particular it will be important to think about the factors that increase the propensity for unsafe risk-taking behaviour as opposed to risk on purpose; this might include pressure from friends, drug or alcohol use, societal or cultural pressures. Young people can experience such pressure to be accepted that they may find it hard to resist the risk. There is also increasing neuro-scientific research evidence around risk-taking and the adolescent brain that suggests that teenagers' brains are extra sensitive to the rewarding feelings they experience when something happens that is better than they anticipated. They are also much more likely to take risks when in the company of other adolescents. This might help explain why young people are more likely to take the kind of risk that most adults avoid, such as taking illegal substances or driving too fast. The potential rewards appear bigger when it comes to risk-taking than the potential for negative outcomes, especially when you factor in that the positive feedback they get from friends may also be contributing to tuning the brain's reward system to be increasingly sensitive to the reward value of risky behaviour (see APS 2013).

It is important to keep the lines of communication open and to remind the young person of his safety network (see *Establishing Personal Networks* on page 64). Talking to or being with an adult may help the young person make safer choices. It can also help to re-direct the young person to activities where risks can be taken in adult-led activities, such as the Scouts or Duke of Edinburgh award scheme.

Sensory Book of Safety

Materials

Pens, good quality paper and some means of tying the pages together to make a book.

Process

Explain that you are going to make a personalised book that captures all those things in the child's life that help him to feel safe. You are then going to explore the things that the child connects with a sense of safety, using all five senses. He will be able to understand the meaning of safety through his sense of touch, smell, sight, taste and sound. You might share some of your own experiences here to help the child conceptualise this activity, and there are many ways to help him connect with his sensory world.

The simplest way is to give the child five worksheets relating to the senses, for example:

I like to see_____; I feel_____when I see.

Or

I like to smell_____and this helps me feel_____.

Or

My safe_____smell, taste, touch, sight, sound is_____.

However, I tend to think this could be too much like school for many children I have worked with, and there are many other ways in which to make this more engaging and experiential. The following is inspired by Lippett (1990, p.17).

TOUCH

- Use a 'feely bag', where the child dips his hand into a bag of objects with different textures and guesses what he is touching. Connect this with what it makes him feel. Objects could include a pine cone, a golf ball, a piece of soft fur/fabric, a seashell, an elastic band or hair bobble.

- Make a tactile collage of items that feel soft and gentle to touch, for example, satin fabric or fur, cotton wool balls.

- Ask the child to bring something from home that feels safe or soothing to touch or have some objects ready to explore together, such as a soft toy, a blanket, a silky clothes tag or a feather.

- Go on a 'trust walk', where the blindfolded child will be led around the room (or in a safe outside space) while you give a verbal tour. Ensure that there are suitable obstacles on the route as well as items with interesting textures. The child is allowed to touch objects he comes into contact with, smell them and try to guess what they are – all using his non-sight senses (see Golding and Todd 1994, p.20).

SMELL

- Play a game of 'Guess the Smell'. Have a series of products on cotton wool balls in plastic pots and see if the child can identify the item. I use a variety of smells including perfume, toothpaste, menthol, lavender or ground coffee.

- Go for a 'smelling' walk outside, and see if you can identify or categorise what you smell. Are there food smells (e.g. as you pass a takeaway), natural smells (like mown grass or flowers), pollution smells (from traffic emissions) or cosmetic smells (perfume, deodorant or make-up)? Of course, you could go for a 'seeing' or 'hearing' walk too.

SIGHT

- Explore the colour spectrum or draw a rainbow and think about the feelings that get attached to different colours.

- Have a selection of magazines to skim through together to look for images that connect with safety for the child – it could be symbolic (a shape, a colour) or a physical object.

TASTE

- Make a mind map of favourite foods and drinks and connect with the feelings they invoke.

- Make a food and drink collage, using dried foods (e.g. pasta, lentils or beans) or images cut out of magazines, images downloaded from the internet and clipart.

- Have a variety of foods to taste across a wide palate range – sweet, sour, salty, spicy – and a range of textures – crunchy, chewy, melt in the mouth. If the child is happy to be blindfolded during this activity, he can also guess what he is tasting. Be careful to ask about allergies first!

- Use stories – I like *The Very Hungry Caterpillar* by Eric Carle (2013). There are lots of resources connected with this story, but the touch and feel board book fits the bill beautifully, especially for younger children.

- Mime the making and tasting of his favourite and least favourite foods.

SOUND

- Make a mood board of sounds that evoke different feelings in the child – you could use clipart images, images from magazines or simply draw the sounds. For example, a scared board might include thunder and lightning or police sirens. A happy board might include the sound of a network person's voice (see *Establishing Personal Networks* on page 64) or a particular song.

- Experiment with musical instruments or listen to a range of different musical styles. Can the child connect a piece of music or a musical sound with a feeling or a sensation in his body?

- Play 'Peanut Butter and Jelly', where the child will copy your tone of voice in repeating the words 'peanut butter' or 'jelly' after you. For example, using a whisper, shouting, wailing, etc.

- Categorise different sounds: machine sounds, household sounds, school sounds, nature sounds, people sounds.

Aims

- To help the child connect with sensory experiences.

- To help the child connect with a sense of safety and create a resource he can come back to when he needs to reconnect with a sense of safety.

- To have some fun!

Handy hints

Depending on how long the child wants to spend exploring and then drawing or decorating each sensory experience, you might finish the book in two minutes or in two hours.

Be mindful here of the child's history. As well as being a comfort, sensory experience can also connect with unconscious, unprocessed traumatic memories that the child might struggle to recognise. Ask parents or carers about any known sensory trauma triggers before starting the activity.

My Safe Place

Materials

Paper and felt tip pens. (Other objects such as pebbles or pine cones, blankets and cushions are optional.)

Process

It is important to support children to create reminders of safety, either in their own imaginations or in a tangible, concrete sense. Using relaxation and visualisation techniques can be a great way of teaching ourselves, and of learning what it feels like to feel and be safe. Tell the child you would like to understand where and how he might feel safe. Ask him to imagine where his safe place could be and to place himself in the centre of this. Some children might be able to close their eyes for a few minutes while they do this; others will feel too vulnerable and unsafe, so use your judgement here.

You might need to offer some prompts to encourage the development of a sense of safety by suggesting it could be somewhere he knows, has been before or a creation from his imagination. Maybe it could connect with a place from a book he has read or a favourite film? Encourage him to think about the sensory elements to this place and to describe them. What can he hear there? What can he see there? What would he taste there? What can he smell there? What would he feel or touch there? What is the weather like there? Is he alone there, or would he like other people or animals alongside him? How does he feel in his body when he is there? This is a good activity to use *after* you have made the *Sensory Book of Safety* (see page 74).

It is really important to guide the child through his journey, especially in the beginning stages. Ask him to take big deep breaths in to relax, and to take in as much of the scene as he can. If you have toys or other materials such as cushions, blankets or tactile fabrics available, feel free to use them to help the child to create his safe space. You could begin the visualisation by saying, 'This is a place where no one can hurt you. You will always be safe here. In your mind, add everything you will need to feel safe in this place.'

Whatever image or visualisation the child creates in his mind, whether based in fantasy or reality, you can return to it whenever you feel the child might need to reconnect with a safe feeling. It is a good idea to identify a 'cue word' or phrase that positively represents his safe place or how he feels in that place. You might also look around for a colour that reminds the child of his safe place when he is ready to return to the world outside of his imagination. He need only look around for that colour, wherever he is, to reconnect with a sense of calm and safety.

A useful extension to this activity would be to ask the child to then draw his safe place. You could photograph or laminate the image so the child can keep this representation of safety with him at home or at school.

Aims

- To help the child connect with a feeling of safety using all his senses. This includes the concept of safety being both internal and external.

- To learn about internal boundaries and to build feelings of trust and safety.

- To learn more about what the child considers a safe place and whether there are any healthy connections to be made with real life.

- To create a tangible representation of safety to use in your work when the sessions become more challenging for the child. Visualising a safe place is a relaxation technique that can help bring down high states of arousal in the child.

Handy hints

Some children may struggle to imagine a safe place without concrete suggestions or prompts. You don't want to create the sense of safety *for* the child because it will then not feel authentic to him, but you also want to avoid the child becoming anxious about the task. There is a balance to be reached between supporting and encouraging and doing *for* the child.

With an older child, you could extend the activity by asking him to imagine other things that can act as agents of safety, such as imagining a force field around his body or breathing in warm and healing energy. You are then teaching the child a technique he can use at other times of stress to ground himself in a sense of safety. The more a young person can practise this technique, the more effective it will be for him.

If you feel the child is struggling with this activity, either becoming cut-off or hyper-aroused, you may need to help ground him in the present. Remind him of where he is, of what he can see and hear around him, and reassure him that he is safe. You could ask him simple questions to bring him back to the here and now, such as 'What are you going to have for tea tonight?' You may also find that giving him something to hold, such as a pebble or piece of Play-Doh or Theraputty, can help this grounding process. Older children and adolescents particularly benefit from having something to occupy their hands, to cover their nervousness and embarrassment, and to help them to relax.

Visualisation can also be used to help the child with overwhelming feelings. Ask the child to imagine what that feeling would look like with as much sensory detail as he can manage about texture, temperature, smell, colour, weight and size, sound, movement, etc. Invite the child to use his 'superpowers' to make whatever changes he would like to this feeling, and when he approves of the new look feeling, encourage him to park it or store it somewhere until he needs it. This is a great way of helping children feel more in control of overwhelming or 'big' feelings (NSPCC 1997, p.106).

Relaxation Techniques

Materials
Cushions and blankets or beanbags would be lovely but are not essential, as well as a quiet, comfortable space in which to sit or lie down, if appropriate. You need a space where you will not be interrupted.

Process
Some children are so hyper-aroused by their environment or hyper-vigilant because of early trauma that they can sometimes confuse strong feelings, in particular, excitement, with sexual feelings. Cavanagh Johnson talks about times when problematic sexual behaviour is the child's unconscious way of reducing 'anxiety, tension or other unpleasant feelings, thoughts or sensations' (1998b, p.5). A child's capacity to make safe choices at these times is also impaired.

It is really important to help these children to achieve a level of control over their arousal levels, and importantly for vulnerable children to learn that this is something they can do *for themselves and can control.* It is not done *to* them. They have control over how deeply they relax and when they stop.

There are many games and activities to help relax the body and the mind. Here is a selection of some of my favourites, but there are many others out there available online for free. I have drawn examples from a beautifully illustrated little book designed for children entitled *Relax* by Catherine O'Neill (1993), and have also added some of my own particular favourites.

BREATHING EXERCISES

Tell the child that as he breathes he is taking in the air his body needs to give him the energy to run, play, talk and sleep. It's just like filling up a car with fuel to keep it running well. When we are tense we don't always breathe properly, and this stops our bodies from working so well. Some breathing exercises to help the child relax are:

- Relaxing rocks: Find smooth stones or pebbles that will easily fit in a little hand. Ask the child to breathe in deeply through his nose, squeezing the stone hard as he does so. As he slowly exhales through his mouth, he can leave all his negative emotion, tension or stress behind in the stone as he also loosens his grip. Repeat.

- Candles: To help the child slow his breathing and feel calmer, ask him to imagine that the tip of his forefinger is a candle. Ask him to take a deep breath in through his nose and to blow out softly and slowly through his mouth so that the candle stays alight and flickers. Repeat.

- Axe: This involves movement and can be helpful in managing strong, negative feelings. Ask the child to imagine he's holding an axe and before him is a large tree trunk that he is going to chop into logs. Get him to hold the axe with two hands, and taking a big breath in through his nose, to raise it above his head. As he brings the axe down to chop the log, the child exhales rapidly. I always encourage the child to make a sound to reflect the effort made – a loud 'huh!' usually works.

- Bowl of soup: Ask the child to imagine he is holding a bowl of his favourite soup in his hands. The soup smells so delicious that he is going to breathe in the aroma, taking a deep breath in through his nose. As the soup is so hot, he will also have to gently blow on it before it is cool enough to taste. So ask him to gently exhale through his mouth, blowing gently so the soup doesn't spill. Liking soup isn't essential for this exercise, though. I've just done it with a girl holding a 'slice of pepperoni pizza…'

- Blowing bubbles: As well as being good fun, blowing bubbles can be a great way of regulating breathing as children are encouraged to take a big breath in and then blow out their worries or troubles into the bubble. As the bubble floats away or disappears, so it takes the child's troubles with it.

- Child's pose: One of the most calming yoga postures is called the child's pose. Ask the child to kneel down on the floor with his bottom resting on his ankles. Ask him then to stretch his arms forwards until his arms and forehead rest on the ground and his tummy rests on his thighs. This is a way of temporarily shutting the external world out and grabbing a few moments of peace and quiet. It's also nice for adults too. When you would like the child to come out of his relaxed state, orientate him to the environment he is in with you – the room you are in, who is present, etc. Invite him to take some deep breaths in and to begin to wiggle his fingers and toes before opening his eyes.

OTHER RELAXATION TECHNIQUES

- Spine: This is good to do if you have the child's parent/carer in the session with you. Ask the child to find his spine or backbone and to feel all the little bones in a long line, stretching from his neck down to his bottom. With the child either sitting on the floor in front of his parent/carer or lying face down on some cushions, ask the parent/carer to run their fingers along these little bones, while the child imagines he is a dinosaur with a tiny mouse tip-toeing down his spine, bone by bone. Alternatively have the child imagine he is a friendly cat or dog who loves to be stroked. Ask the parent/carer to gently stroke the child's back from the neck down, along his spine, soothing away tension.

- Feet, legs, bottom, tummy, arms: This is another good exercise to try if you have a parent/carer present. Ask the parent/carer to wrap the child in a blanket and get comfortable either lying on some cushions or on his knee. Have the parent/carer talk the child gently through relaxing each part of his body. Begin by telling the child: 'Think first of your feet, let them go soft and floppy or relaxed and heavy. They are so relaxed you can't lift them up. Imagine them in a bowl of lovely warm water.' Then the child should be encouraged to imagine this comforting, warm feeling spreading through his body. Next let his hands feel tingly, and then his arms and so on, as you gradually work around his body.

- Hands: Tell the child 'Squeeze your hands into a tight ball, pretending to hold onto something that is very precious to you. Squeeze really tight and don't drop it! Now stretch open your hands, spreading your fingers wide and making them grow longer and longer. Now drop your hands until they become really heavy and are falling to the floor.' As you play, you can create a picture in your mind. Imagine your tight fist has become a flower bud that is opening slowly in the warm, summer sunshine. As the sun sets, the flower closes again.

- Massage: With a carer/parent present, you could ask them to massage the child's hands or feet with baby lotion or hand cream. I like to then make a hand or footprint that is sprinkled with talcum powder to make a lasting image the child can take home that represents both nurture and relaxation.

- Slow motion movement: Encourage the child to practise making movements in slow motion, for example, running, swimming, scoring a goal in football or shaking hands. You and the parent/carer could also have a go. You can also move on to expressing feelings in slow motion. This is a good exercise to help with regulation for the child who becomes quickly hyper-aroused or can be impulsive and easily distractible in the session. My favourite suggestion from one boy was to do the slow motion 'Cha cha cha'!

Aims

- To teach the child simple techniques to self-soothe and relax his mind and body, especially at times of stress and anxiety.

- To reassure the child that you and his parent/carer can help him regulate if his feelings become overwhelming during the sessions.

- To build on the attachment relationship between the child and his parent/carer, and provide opportunities for nurture and engagement.

Handy hints

Sunderland (2006, p.46) reminds us that, 'in order to activate the calm and centred branch in your child's autonomic nervous system, you need to quieten yourself down first... As soon as you do some effective deep breathing, your whole system will calm, and your body will send messages to your brain, telling it to stop pumping out high levels of stress hormones.'

Before introducing any relaxation exercises you might instead get the child to practise listening to music for a couple of minutes, sitting quietly, with his eyes closed. Even then, some children may experience difficulties with closing their eyes to relax, as it can feel incredibly risky. You could gently and quietly encourage the child to try shutting his eyes for a few seconds at a time, gradually increasing his tolerance if possible, but for some children this is just too much, and you should accept that. A problem can also arise if the child squeezes his eyes too tightly shut, thereby increasing tension in the face. He might be trying too hard or be feeling very apprehensive or afraid. Give the reminder to gently and slowly close the eyes.

Other children find it hard to get into a comfortable position to sit or lie down. Generally, though, sitting down leads to less fidgeting than lying down. If appropriate, the parent/carer might gently lay a hand on the restless body part and stay close by until the child can relax a little better (see Rickard 1996, pp.9–10).

Encourages 'practise, practise, practise' at home so the child learns what it feels like to have a relaxed body and mind. This will not happen overnight, so be sure to remind parents/carers of this. You can also use these techniques in future sessions if you feel the subject matter is becoming overwhelming for the child.

The Mr Men story *Mr Jelly* by Roger Hargreaves (2007) is another good resource for younger children as you can talk about how Mr Jelly uses counting and breathing exercises to help him to relax and to think more clearly.

A final note of caution relates to using breathing techniques with children with respiratory problems such as asthma, or children who have experienced trauma or medical interventions with breathing, such as assisted ventilation.

Tuning in to Your Body

Materials

A comfortable, quiet space to sit, with enough room to do some physical exercise on the spot; a stopwatch or timer, pen and paper.

Process

Blaustein and Kinniburgh (2010, p.280) suggest these activities in relation to affect modulation. In effect this is about making connections between feelings the child experiences in his body and how he then manages them. They can be done with individuals or in a group. The idea is to demonstrate that in order to regulate your body, you need to be able to tune in and notice where you are in the here and now. Although the body responds automatically to different cues and experiences, there are positive things you can do to change your arousal level.

First, ask the child to measure his heartbeat. Teach him how to take his pulse by putting his index finger on his wrist or neck – don't use the thumb. Have him count for 20 seconds then multiply by three to get a baseline pulse rate. Write this down. Then have the child do some exercise, for example, 10–15 star jumps or jog on the spot for 30 seconds. Immediately after stopping, re-measure the pulse rate and again write it down. Finally, encourage the child to take five deep breaths sitting down, in through the nose and slowly out through the mouth. After the deep breaths, re-measure the pulse rate and write it down.

You can think together about up-regulation and down-regulation. How did his heartbeat change across the three activities? Did he notice any other changes in his body when his heartbeat sped up and slowed down again? Were the breathing exercises effective in slowing down his heart rate? If not, why?

Aims

- To increase awareness of the child's own physiological arousal.

- To look at how different activities affect arousal levels.

Handy hints

It's fine to substitute alternatives for both up- and down-regulation to suit the child or young person. Look at the exercises in *Relaxation Techniques* on page 80 for inspiration.

Physical activity can also help children and young people cope with big feelings and to manage their energy levels. Depending on the individual, some activities will lower the body's arousal levels and others will increase it. You can explore different activities with the child to track energy/arousal levels. Perhaps use a scaling tool to help you with this. For example, on a scale of 1:10, where 1 represents low energy and 10 the highest energy, ask the child to let you know where he is on the scale before, during and after exercise. Energy (arousal) can be high, medium or low. The child should look for clues in his body to help him understand his energy levels, for example, is he feeling hot or cold (temperature)? Is his heartbeat fast or slow? Is his breathing fast or slow? And are his muscles tense or relaxed?

Chapter 4

Body Awareness
and Boundaries

Introduction

Most animals are territorial; those of us with a pet cat or dog will have
observed them marking territory, both inside and outside the house.
Other animals will set boundaries around their dens or nests to keep
danger away. A human's home territory is also of great importance of
course, and we manage the delineation of other territories through
fencing or signage. However, for most people, it is our personal space
that holds more importance than our territorial space: 'Personal space
refers to a portable territory we all carry around with us' (Nowicki
and Marshall 1992, pp.43–44). It can be seen as a flexible bubble
that surrounds us and that contracts or expands depending on the
situation or people we are with.

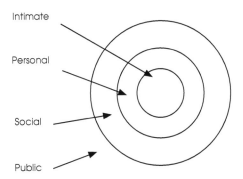

Inside this bubble are four zones in which different kinds of communication take place, and it is important in terms of building safety and keeping safe to support vulnerable children and young people to understand the rules of these zones. The *intimate* zone is where we allow close friends and family to interact and relate to us. The *personal* zone extends further out, and this is where we have conversations with friends and acquaintances in everyday settings, such as school or work. The *social* zone is one in which it is okay to use a louder voice and where we may be engaging with people we have just met. There's a good chance other people will overhear conversations in this zone, so it is not a good place to talk about personal or private matters. The final zone is the largest, and is known as the *public* zone. We don't usually talk to people in this zone, and communication is usually non-verbal or using gestures. Although researchers have set limits around the size of each of these zones, it is fair to say that there are also some cultural variations.

Most of us follow these space rules every day without even thinking about it. We naturally assimilate them as we grow, and as we observe the boundaries being upheld and modelled initially by our parents/carers:

> A child's capacity to organize and interpret reality effectively is strongly influenced by the development of a healthy boundary system. The boundaries that we develop affect how we process and respond to information and experiences about ourselves, others, and the surrounding world. Until children learn to negotiate their own boundary systems, their parents act as their external regulators. (Grotsky *et al.* 2000, p.99)

However, in families where parents may not have had good interpersonal boundaries themselves, they often fail to prioritise teaching these vital life skills to their children. Without parents acting as their external regulators, children fail to learn that everybody needs their own emotional, physical and sexual space, and must learn to respect the needs of others. Cavanagh Johnson uses the helpful metaphor of a 'space invader' (1998a, p.18) for someone who encroaches on another person's boundaries. Space invasion occurs regularly in the homes of vulnerable children in diverse ways. Although the boundaries of acceptable behaviour with regard to privacy vary according to individual family rules and in some cases cultural norms, for some children the rules are further blurred because they may change depending on who is in charge or whose privacy is being protected. This lack of clarity leads to confusion.

I'm sure most readers will be able to easily call to mind those children and young people who haven't yet learned about boundaries and body awareness. They stand too close, are 'in our faces', or try to hug us or sit on our knees on first meeting. These children are not clear that they are using the intimate zone rather than the preferred personal or social zone. Other children might talk too loudly at the social zone distance, perhaps in the playground or at lunch break where others can overhear, about personal or family matters that would best be discussed in the privacy of the intimate zone. I have heard tales of children loudly asking their foster carers questions about their abuse history at the supermarket checkout. I know children who will indiscriminately share painful personal details about coming into the care of the local authority with peers in school or who will try to forge intense, exclusive friendships with children they have just met. Although children are generally given more leeway with these space rules than adults, who will be expected to have learned them, they can still often experience peer rejection and social isolation when they repeatedly breach the rules. They are also potentially more vulnerable to victimisation if they don't recognise social boundaries and respect personal space, and they therefore need support to learn these vital skills.

It is normal that as individuals grow, the amount of personal space they need changes over time. An infant who needs to be held by an adult, soothed, changed and nursed, has different needs to a toddler who may sometimes need to be carried, but who can walk independently, through to an adolescent who would rather not even be in the same room as his parent/carer! In some families these natural processes of change as the child matures may be delayed because of the needs of the adults. For example, parents may continue to bathe their children long after they are able to do so independently, or bring the child into their bed because the parent/carer doesn't like sleeping alone.

As well as being the earliest way we have of making contact with others, touch is essential to our healthy development. In addition to being fundamental to an infant's survival in terms of receiving the biological essentials for life, we all need to be touched and held to know we are loved and cared for. Yet even here, there are cultural variations, with British people and Americans being some of the least likely cultures to touch or be touched. Touching rules are complex, especially for children who are not taught the basics by their parents/ carers. There is, in essence, a vocabulary of touch, with general agreements about where it is acceptable to touch another person.

In children who have experienced relational trauma, however, it is common to see problems with expressive and receptive touch. Children with expressive touch difficulties can struggle to keep their hands to themselves and touch others and sometimes themselves inappropriately. They are the children who will indiscriminately approach strangers in the park or cafe, and will act as if they've known them forever. Children with receptive touch difficulties will not allow others to touch them – even gentle, sensitive attempts to provide comfort or care are quickly rejected, and the child will withdraw. These children who are incredibly resistant to touch lose out on the benefits the right kind of physical touch can bring. Where children have experienced sexual abuse by someone they know well, they are more vulnerable to learning that physical closeness equates to sexual behaviour. Consequently 'overt, compulsive or unusual sexual behaviours in children can be conditioned responses to previous abuse and/or habitual reactions to anxiety' (Brohl 1996, p.29). It is imperative that we support these children in learning new boundaries and in experiencing safe touch.

Any form of warm, physical contact between the child and parent/ carer can bring such positive effects, activating opioids and oxytocin (feel-good hormones) in the child's brain, especially with under-fives. Sunderland (2006, p.89) stresses the importance of the amazing brain effects of touch with older children and young people too:

> If you keep lots of lovely cuddles going right through into adolescence (as long as the young person still wants them from you, of course), there can be far less tension in your relationship when your children become teenagers. This is because the oxytocin from the cuddles will keep the opioid bond with your child alive for far longer.

It is also important to note that touch has diverse meanings in different cultures and communities. While in some cultures people only hug or kiss close family, in others this may extend to friends or acquaintances. There are additional nuances relating to how close people stand to each other, how they shake hands or the nature of the embrace (two kisses on the cheek or three?) While we must be aware of different cultural norms, however, culture can never be used as an excuse to justify abusive behaviour towards children – children have a right to feel and be safe regardless of their ethnic or cultural background.

Some issues raised by Lord Laming (in his inquiry into the death of Victoria Climbié; see DH 2009, pp.34–35) to consider when working with children and families from different cultural backgrounds are:

- Be aware of your own assumptions, culture and stereotypes, and think how these could affect a child you are working with.

- Do not assume that families of a particular ethnicity conform to specific beliefs and practices. Do not make judgements about a family's lifestyle based on generalisations about a particular race or culture.

- Cultural beliefs such as izzat and sharam (honour and shame) may act as barriers to some families accessing services.

- There may be poor communication due to a language barrier; ensure you mitigate against this by providing a good interpreting service.

We also need to consider that children with disabilities who qualify as vulnerable children in need under Section 17(10) of the Children Act 1989 are three times more likely to be abused than non-disabled children, and learning disabled children are 3.4 times more likely to be abused or neglected (Sullivan and Knutson 2000). Body awareness and boundary issues are especially relevant for this group of children and young people, and there are three primary reasons for this. First, the disability may make it harder to report the abuse or stop the abuse from happening, particularly where there are communication difficulties. Second, there are inadequate services in some areas to support families of children with disabilities that can stretch some parents to breaking point. And third, societal attitudes and assumptions about children with disabilities can prevent abuse from being identified and support being offered. Any emotional or behavioural concerns that may be abuse-related are automatically connected with the disability, and alternative understandings are not always sought.

There are other issues that increase vulnerability for children with disabilities (see DH 2009, pp.35–37):

- children with disabilities may be less able to avoid abusive situations

- they may have communication difficulties that make disclosure harder

- they may receive intimate care from a number of different adults – professional carers, teaching staff and family members – which increases their exposure to potentially abusive situations

- they may have less opportunities for contact with people out of the family home where access to social or leisure opportunities is limited.

The activities in this chapter are designed to support children to learn their rights and responsibilities in relation both to themselves and to other people. You will find activities relating to external boundaries that raise issues around personal space, physical touch and psychological distance. Simple things such as looking at photographs of the child at different ages, saying what you see in the mirror, mirror movements or movement to music can also help with this. When the child has an understanding of and can practise good external boundaries, you can introduce the idea of internal boundaries – this involves the identification and processing of feelings, thoughts and beliefs that will help children make better choices about behaviour. There are further activities to support this in Chapter 2.

Healthy Touching House Rules

Materials
Paper and felt tip pens.

Process

This is a good joint activity to do with the child's parent/carer. Make an image or poster to depict the house rules on which they reach agreement. The areas you need to explore may include the following, but will be different in every household:

- personal space around the body

- private space to keep things you might not want to share

- right to privacy in the bathroom, for getting dressed and sleeping alone in bed

- private parts of the body

- private thoughts.

You will also want to encourage the development of healthy physical and emotional contact at home, especially where there is a physical or sexual abuse history – comforting and soothing touch that meets a basic human need and open, respectful communication between family members. You might want to make a list of healthy family touches too, for children where there is a need to be very explicit about what is okay and what is not okay. For example, washing or brushing hair, shaking hands, giving a 'high five', patting someone's back or shoulder, holding hands, a younger child sitting on a parent/carer's knee.

Remember that natural and healthy physical contact is vital for the healthy development of children and young people, but where boundaries have been violated by abusive experiences, children may not recognise healthy boundaries and need help to learn them. It is important in these situations that children have the opportunity to practise receiving nurturing, non-sexual touch where they have an element of control over the type of physical contact received.

Aims

- To encourage the development of healthy rules in the home around privacy and space.

- To encourage children to understand what they can expect from others in relation to their rights around healthy physical, sexual and emotional boundaries.

Handy hints

It is imperative that adults are absolutely clear and consistent with children about which behaviours are acceptable and which are not. Some behaviours might be cute or funny in certain contexts or at a very young age, but then children end up confused when the same behaviours are punished in another setting, at another time or by another adult. We cannot expect children to make good decisions about time, place and person, and must do that for them consistently and predictably if they are to learn the rules.

My Own Space

Materials

A comfortable, quiet space to lie in and/or paper and felt tip pens.

Process

The object of this activity is to support the child to create his own physical, seeing, hearing and mind space in order to be able to stay in his own space to be calm and peaceful. First, explain that we all have the right to our own physical space where we cannot touch anyone else and cannot be touched. We also sometimes need our own hearing space where we cannot hear others or make noises that will enter someone else's space. Finally, we need our own seeing space where we are not distracted and do not distract other people. The best way to achieve this is to gently close our eyes. We need our own mind space where we don't have to think or worry about everyday things, and we can try to make our mind clear (see Rickard 1996, p.23).

Ask the child to find his own space in the room where he can either sit or lie down. Make sure he is comfortable – leaning against something may make his body stiffen. If he lies down, make sure it is flat on his back, on his tummy or on one side. The child should focus on the breath coming in and out of the body and on making connections with sensory experience.

Aim

- To help the child develop a sense of his own space in which he can be calm, peaceful and feel safe.

Handy hints

Expand this activity as you might for the *My Safe Place* visualisation (on page 77) in order to access all the senses. If the child is uncomfortable with accessing the physical safe space, you could suggest making a visual representation through image making. Some children might benefit from some breathing or relaxation exercises in order to make best use of this exercise (see *Relaxation Techniques*, page 80).

Animal Boundaries

Materials

None – just a large, comfortable room.

Process

This a great activity for younger children with a good imagination. It's a playful way to teach children that their thoughts, feelings and bodily sensations impact their behaviour. When children have an understanding of this premise, it is easier to help them learn they have more control and choice over their actions. It can work well with sibling groups.

First, ask the child to close his eyes (if the child feels safe to do so) and to imagine he is an animal. Lead the child through a guided visualisation asking questions only to be answered in his mind. Questions might include:

- Is it a friendly or a fierce animal?

- Is it a baby animal or fully grown?

- What are the animal's strengths?

- How big is the animal?

- Does it have fur, feathers or scales?

Then ask the child (or children in turn) to act out, using his body, how his animal would react in different scenarios. You could either act the part of the human yourself, or ask another child to do so, but touch in these role-plays should always be pretend. Examples might include:

- If the animal is scared, happy, afraid, excited, etc.

- If the animal is being stroked gently.

- If the animal has been locked in a cage.

- If someone has pulled the animal's tail.

Aim to finish with a positive feeling, and then explore the ways in which how we feel on the inside affects how we look and act on the outside. You can connect this with the child's own experiences. How does he act when he is really hungry – is he more impatient or irritable? How does he act when he is tired but really wants to play out a while longer? How does he act the night before something exciting is going to happen, like a holiday or birthday party?

The final extension to this activity would be to reflect on boundary issues in the scenarios you played out for the animal characters. For example, how did the cat tell the human he didn't like having his tail pulled? Did he hiss, scratch or run away? What about the rabbit who didn't want to be stroked? You can then extend this further to look at how the child would respond to unkind, inappropriate or unwanted touch. How would he show his boundary if someone hugged him and he didn't like it? What words would he use? What would he do with his body to show he didn't want to be touched? This is an opportunity to also explore the differences between an assertive or an aggressive response.

Aims

- To learn about internal and external boundaries.

- To learn to manage personal triggers.

- To increase the child's ability to identify and express feelings safely.

- To increase the child's capacity to identify felt sensations in the body and to understand what they might mean.

- To teach how feelings and thoughts affect behaviour.

Handy hints

Although children usually like this activity, you need to keep it moving and not spend too much time talking, as they can soon become distracted. It also helps to reinforce the safety boundaries and remind the child to keep his animal under control, especially if provoked!

The Boundary Line

Materials

None – just a reasonably large room with space to move about.

Process

This activity is adapted from Grotsky *et al.* (2000, pp.103–105), and works best in groups or when working with a family or sibling group for children of all ages. It is popular in self-defence classes as it teaches children to pay attention to their inside feelings and to connect with their bodies to make better choices about safety.

Begin by asking everyone to imagine they are all strangers, and divide them into two groups on opposite sides of the room, standing in a line, facing each other, with about a 5-metre space separating them. It then helps if you demonstrate the next steps either with a co-worker or a willing volunteer. One person stands still while the other slowly walks towards him. The stationary person tells the other to stop when she notices herself beginning to feel uncomfortable. She will then hold out an arm to gauge how much space she needs in order to feel safe. It might be one arm's length for some people or three arms' lengths for others. You could use paper plate feelings faces to help illustrate when the distance feels comfortable (happy face) or when the distance feels too close (sad face). The stationary person can control how close the other worker comes by switching from the happy to sad feelings face when the other person has come too near.

Give the two lines a name – a simple 'A' and 'B' will suffice. Get the As to walk towards the Bs and the Bs to shout 'stop' or change their feeling face when being any closer wouldn't feel okay. Take some time to discuss how the Bs decided the As were close enough. How did the As know what the Bs were feeling? Did any As want the Bs to shout 'stop' sooner? Did the Bs do anything to let the As know to stop?

You can mix up the lines so everyone is opposite somebody new, and then repeat the activity. There are other variations to this scenario with the boundary lines to help children learn that their personal boundaries might change in different settings. You could experiment with the person approaching being a friend, stranger, favourite teacher, someone you feel cross with, someone you love, or for older adolescents, someone who is drunk or who has taken drugs.

Aims

- To help the child learn about external boundaries.

- To help assess the child's sense of personal safety with others in the session.

- To introduce the idea of rights and responsibilities in relation to having a body that is precious and that deserves protection and care.

- To increase the child's ability to express his personal needs.

- To identify when someone is physically too close to another person, and to explore how that person might feel.

Handy hints

This works best when the child is able to take it seriously and not get too giggly or playful with saying 'stop'. If saying 'stop' is difficult, experiment with alternative statements such as 'no' or 'get away'. You might need to pause the activity to practise saying these words firmly, loudly and assertively, and to get the giggling out of the way!

Gadd and Hinchliffe (2007, pp.42–43) use a comparable activity with young people with moderate to severe learning disabilities, and practise techniques for communicating with someone who is too close. They use an image of a couple hugging, explaining that the boy, 'Matt', had to agree to hug the girl, 'Jess', and to be that close to each other. They would then think about what might happen if we hug someone who doesn't want to be hugged. They use active methods of exploring how big their personal space is in the room – gently moving their arms and legs about to see what area they can cover. If you do this, make certain that the young person has found a big enough space not to be connecting with other people, walls or furniture in the room. A foster carer I worked with used the 'hula hoop rule' to explain that your personal space is the area that would be inside a hula hoop around your waist.

Body Tracing

Materials
Felt tip coloured pens and a roll of lining paper.

Process
This activity introduces the child to the idea of identifying personal boundaries, being aware of his body, and expressing what it is okay and not okay to touch. Either draw around the child's body, ensuring he is comfortable by checking in as you do so, or use a body template. Focus the child on his body safety needs as you do this. Then explain that you will be using a colour code to demonstrate personal safety needs on the body outline. You can offer a key or let the child choose his own. An example of a key might be:

Green = everywhere I like to be touched.

Red = everywhere I don't like to be touched.

Purple = the parts where I'm not bothered if I'm touched.

Blue = the parts only I can touch.

Aims

- To define age-appropriate sexual behaviour/touch.

- To build self-protection skills and a healthy body image.

- To increase the child's capacity to define and express his safety needs.

- To introduce the idea of the right to have a body to protect and to keep safe.

Handy hints

Not all children will feel comfortable with having you draw around their bodies, even if you stress that they won't be touched. Conversely, some children may seem too comfortable. Always hold in your mind the option of drawing the body free hand on a wallpaper roll or of using a small body outline. Also be sure to consider cultural attitudes to different body parts and the impact on children with a poor body image or sensitivity to body shape or size. Remember that you can draw around the body with the child lying on the floor or you can pin the paper to the wall and draw around the body with the child standing up, if this feels safer.

When you get started, you might need to offer gentle prompts to check the child is changing colour for different areas, as they can sometimes just get carried away.

If you have the child's parent/carer with you during the session, it might be nice to end with a hand or foot massage to support reinforcement of positive and nurturing touch.

Private versus Public Spaces and Places

Materials

Felt tip pens and a large sheet of paper. You could bring photographs or clip art images to help with this activity to use rather than writing and drawing, for example, images of public and private places (bedroom, bathroom, park, school); people taking part in different activities including chatting, hugging; a male and female fully dressed, in underwear, naked; and different body parts.

Process

It is important to teach children from a young age (toddler and pre-school) the correct names for body parts, and that 'private' means parts of his body that only he should touch (with a few exceptions that are expanded upon on page 102 in *Private and Public Parts of the Body*). Kehoe (1988, p.11) helpfully talks about teaching 'children to be on a first name basis with their bodies'. When we are talking about private places on the body, it's often helpful for children to think about the places that would be covered by swimming costumes or underwear, and also to include the mouth area.

Many of us, perhaps because of our own discomfort, have fallen into the trap of using other terminology to describe the genitals – 'bits and bobs', 'Mary', 'foo foo', to name but a few I've heard used. Aside from the message this gives children that genitals cannot be politely discussed without using a pseudonym, there are also possible implications for future disclosures of sexual harm, when children's statements or evidential interviews can lack clarity – there is a difference between a child saying: 'X touched me on my cookie' and 'X touched me on my vagina'. A child using the correct anatomical names for the genitalia is more likely to be listened to and taken seriously. In addition to this, a child who tells a perpetrator, 'Stop, don't touch my vagina', identifies herself as a child with good body safety knowledge.

However, for some children and adults, talking about private parts can be excruciating (even though there are some great resources to help), so it is sometimes easier to start by talking about the concepts of *public* and *private* in more general terms.

For this activity, take a large sheet of paper and fold it into quarters, giving each section a title (see below), and then either drawing or writing a further exploration of each. If you have prepared cards/ images, ask the child to decide for each image if it is public or private, and place it in the correct quadrant. You might need to start off by giving an example.

PRIVATE AND PUBLIC ROOMS OR SPACES

Private places are where one person or sometimes more than one person can go where others won't disturb them, and they can have more control over who can be there. In the home, the private rooms would be the bathroom/toilet and bedroom, but only if the person is alone in it. They are private for private behaviours such as sleeping, using the toilet and washing.

Public places are where more than one person can be at a time and we have less control over how many people can be there. Some places can be public or private at different times.

PRIVATE AND PUBLIC BEHAVIOURS
AND BODILY FUNCTIONS

Certain behaviours should be private such as burping, going to the toilet, passing wind or masturbating. They should be done in a private room, when the person is alone. You might show some activity cards here – for some young people this could include sexual activity, such as masturbation or having sex. You can then discuss whether the activity would be acceptable in a public or private place. For example, would this be okay in a supermarket?

Be sure on your activity cards to have some public behaviours that would be acceptable in some settings or that will initiate debate. Debate is good! For example, yawning, holding hands with a parent/carer, eating a meal.

PRIVATE AND PUBLIC CLOTHING

Private clothing covers your private parts, such as knickers or underpants, vest or bra, and is covered by public clothes, for example, trousers and t-shirt or a dress or skirt.

PRIVATE AND PUBLIC PARTS OF THE BODY

Private body parts are the bottom, breasts, vagina, penis and mouth. This means that only the child should touch these areas, with a few exceptions – and talk some of these through. For example, a baby having his nappy changed, a doctor's examination, a parent putting cream on a child's sore bottom. If it is absolutely necessary for someone to examine or touch a child's private body parts, they must first ask permission. We need to be clear with children that if you are under 16, even at the GP surgery you should not be examined without another safe adult present.

You might have some images of different people (e.g. doctor, dentist, fireman, police officer, teacher, parent, other child) to show the child to help facilitate this conversation – ask who might be able to touch or see your private or public places, and in what context.

It is also important to talk explicitly about public parts of the body and to discuss in what situations it would be appropriate to show public parts of the body or to be touched on those public parts of the body. This is not clear-cut either. For example, if you are pushing through a crowd or standing on a busy bus or train, it is possible your arms or back might be touched by people you don't know. In that setting this might be acceptable or unavoidable. However, you might feel very differently about a stranger at the park or in the supermarket taking hold of your hand or rubbing your back for no obvious reason.

Aims

- To develop the child's understanding of private and public.

- To develop an accurate vocabulary for talking about private parts of the body.

- To teach the child which activities are appropriate in private or public places.

Handy hints

The best way to teach and reinforce these concepts is through everyday experience; it would be foolish to think any child, especially one for whom the boundaries of private and public have already been repeatedly violated, would fully integrate these messages after one session. When you are bathing younger children or getting them dressed, it is a great time for teaching through experience, but be sure then to connect with other scenarios so the learning isn't just situation-specific. For example, talk about the rules about getting dressed or using the toilet at home, at school and when visiting a friend or relative's home.

Gadd and Hinchliffe (2007, p.39) use a similar activity with young people with moderate to severe learning disabilities, and always use visual prompts to support learning. Although they talk about discussions taking place, they are keen to stress that 'when working with largely non-verbal groups these discussions are more likely to mean an explanation by the facilitator using whatever communication methods are necessary, for example Makaton, Board Maker or other visual aids'. They also suggest using pictures of red crosses or green ticks for young people to indicate if something is acceptable or not. Similarly, I have sometimes used images of thumbs up or thumbs down.

There are also some great children's books that will support increased understanding. *My Body Belongs to Me from My Head to My Toes* (Geisler 2014) is an educational tool to help instil confidence in children when it comes to their bodies. The narrative of the story is led by a girl named 'Clara' who encourages children to say 'no' if they are uncomfortable with physical contact. The narrator gives readers tips about what they can say or do to avoid unwanted physical contact, or how to tell the right people in the event it has already occurred.

Robie H. Harris has written a number of books for different age groups including *It's Not the Stork: A Book about Girls, Boys, Babies, Bodies, Families and Friends* (2008). They all feature clear, straightforward factual information combined with humorous cartoon images and candid questions. This one contains a very short passage about appropriate boundaries for touch and personal privacy. *Let's Talk about Where Babies Come From* (Harris 2004) is another child-friendly book that answers the many normal questions children may have about babies, bodies, love, sex, reproduction and families.

Another extension activity (or alternative starting point) would be for the child to consider different body parts and to fill them in with ideas based on the following questions (see Schonveld and Myko 1999):

Head	What do I think about?
Hands	What do I like to do?
Feet	Where do I like to go?
Heart	Who is special to me?
Arms	Who do I like to hug or keep close?

Exploring Touch

Materials

A large sheet of paper/wallpaper and felt tip pens.

Process

Draw a continuum of touching experiences along the paper from left to right that includes comforting/soothing, taking care of, playful, accidental, neutral, no touch, confusing, harmful or hurtful. Some children might respond better to this if you have images to illustrate the categories, and these are easily found using images downloaded from the internet or clip art. If you laminate the images, you can then re-use them.

First, encourage the child to describe different touches he has experienced that fit these categories, and write them under the headings yourself, or let the child if he chooses. Children may need some support or prompting to bring examples that relate to themselves – you can help with this by asking more specific questions about touches from people they know – parents or carers, friends, teachers or medics.

Where the child is still struggling, you might have to prompt further still by offering a set of different scenarios and asking the child to locate them on the continuum. If it helps you feel more prepared, you can make some examples on cards in advance of the session, and then ask the child to place them on the line. Examples might include playing tag or rugby, applying a plaster or bandage, brushing hair, holding hands, changing a baby's nappy, or accidentally bumping into someone. You might develop this when the time feels right to include things like masturbation, putting cream on genitals when sore, a doctor examining genitals, an adult touching a child's genitals, a child touching a same-aged child's genitals, etc.

Make sure you also talk about a *lack* of touch in different scenarios, and how this impacts on wellbeing, particularly as children who may have experienced absent or neglectful parenting or who have been denied physical or emotional affection are often more vulnerable to sexual abuse.

You can also extend this activity to ask children to match feelings to different touches, initially keeping the emphasis on positive or neutral touch. This can be a complex area for children who have already experienced sexual harm and who will need a sensitive approach. Think about some of these questions to help you explore this area with the child:

- Can your feelings help you decide which touch should go in which category?

- Can you have different feelings about the same kind of touch – perhaps depending on who is doing the touching or the context?

- Do hugs feel different from different people?

- Can you sometimes have positive feelings about negative touch?

One of the greatest challenges for children and young people who have experienced sexual abuse in the context of a 'loving relationship' is to come to terms with the fact that they may have experienced arousal or pleasure during sexual contact that they may later learn is 'bad' or indeed illegal. It will be important to talk about where sexual touching comes on the continuum, as in reality it could span all the categories. You might also need to do some psycho-educative work around the body's normal biological responses to stimulation.

Aims

- To support the child to understand the differences between comforting/soothing touch, touch that is used to take care, accidental touch, neutral touch, no touch, confusing touch and harmful touch along a continuum.

- To understand the difference in touch between children, child and adolescent, child and adult, child and animal.

- To help the child connect with touch as a pleasurable experience and not necessarily with sexuality.

- To help the child understand his rights in relation to touch and to ask for help when he is touched in a confusing or harmful way.

Handy hints

This is an adaptation of an activity from *Treatment Exercises for Child Abuse Victims and Children with Sexual Behaviour Problems* (Cavanagh Johnson 1998a, pp.75–78). Cavanagh Johnson uses this to support children who have been victims of harm and/or who have sexually harmful behaviour towards others. She talks about the need to redress the balance in terms of unhelpful connotations between touch and sex or touch and negative outcomes, and reminds us of the normality of sexual curiosity and a whole range of touching that is normative behaviour in children. When children can independently differentiate between different kinds of touch in different contexts, they will develop the capacity to understand the feelings that are aroused by touch.

If you are doing this activity with a younger child, it might be advisable to limit the number of categories you are exploring. You can use this activity in individual sessions, group work or in family sessions. Depending on the capacity of the child to engage and to tolerate the subject, you may decide to focus initially on the more positive experiences of touch before moving to more difficult stories in subsequent sessions.

Responding to Action Words

Materials

None – just enough room to move around freely.

Process

Make sure the child has enough space around him to freely move around the room without banging in to any furniture. Explain that when you call out a body part and an action word, he must concentrate hard on using that part of his body to do the action. This list will give you some ideas about possible combinations (see Golding and Todd 1994, pp.24–25):

Whole body:	jump	hop	skip	bend
	climb	float	wiggle	flop
Legs:	bounce	jump	crawl	march
	stomp	limp	stumble	dance
Arms:	chop	dig	sweep	brush hair
	lift	stretch	shake	hammer
Hands:	stroke	pat	catch	click fingers
	knock	tickle	scratch	clap
Face:	smile	snarl	frown	blink
	laugh	smirk	yawn	stick tongue out

Aims

- To develop personal body awareness.

- To explore the relationship between movement and different body parts.

- To connect the child with his own body.

Handy hints

Follow up this activity with a discussion around different kinds of communication – verbal and non-verbal.

This can be a good activity to do with overactive or restless children as it allows for movement. It can also be helpful for children for whom there seems to be a disconnect from their bodily experience. This can be common where children's bodies have been violated in abuse situations or where they have experienced traumatic medical procedures or hospitalisation.

You could also blow bubbles and instruct the child to pop them as fast as possible, only using the part of his body that you shout out, for example, head, left arm, right elbow.

Another adaptation of this activity is to play 'Freeze It' (Golding and Todd 1994, p.25). Have the child move around the room in a variety of styles – fast, slow, crawling, wiggling. On a given command, they have to freeze. If you have a larger group you can play this like 'Statues', where if anyone moves, they're out of the game.

Chapter 5

Developing Problem-solving Skills

Introduction

In our everyday lives at home, at work and at school, we are often being challenged with problems to solve. For children and young people, these challenges may relate to family relationships, school achievement, friendships, self-concept or identity. It is simple for some to rise to the challenges and see them as opportunities for development and learning. They may have learned a logical, systematic way of overcoming problems. Repeated success in solving these problems results in greater self-confidence and contributes to developing self-esteem; it also makes you more likely to embrace future challenges and anticipate that you will achieve your goals. Research on resilience also supports the importance of problem-solving skills in positive outcomes for young people (Cicchetti *et al.* 1993; Werner and Smith 2001).

Ultimately our goal in this phase of work should be for children and young people to build their own internal and external resources in order to be able to function healthily. In this chapter, the focus is on activities that 'highlight the importance of children achieving felt mastery and success, receiving tools to continue functioning as active constructors of their lives; and developing and consolidating a positive and coherent sense of self' (Blaustein and Kinniburgh 2010, p.40).

This is so important for vulnerable children and young people, who may not have developed a sense of agency and who do not feel that they have the capacity to make an impact on the world. This only develops as we see, we do and we choose, and to an extent is dependent on the development of the higher executive functions of the brain. Where children have experienced developmental trauma, this can negatively impact the development of the pre-frontal cortex (responsible for impulse control, anticipating consequences, active decision-making, etc.), as the brain's resources are focused on survival – its alarm mode is being constantly triggered by traumatic experiences.

Such children may become anxious or overwhelmed when faced with challenges. They may have little or no way of knowing how to deal with a problem, no matter how minor or trivial it may seem. If you struggle to work out the nature of the problem, it is so much harder to apply the correct analytical tools to solve it. If you repeatedly experience failure in problem-solving, you can soon begin to feel like a failure yourself. Children who lack problem-solving skills may avoid doing anything at all to try to address the issue for themselves.

Other children and young people who lack problem-solving skills may not even know that they have the capacity to make a choice. Without an awareness of options, these children are liable to act impulsively or aggressively rather than assertively or proactively. We need to encourage children to consider all their options, knowing that behavioural choices can have both positive and negative consequences for us all. It is important for children and young people to learn these skills in everyday life without an adult always rushing in to solve the problem for them. Where it is safe to do so, we need sometimes to hold back…to give the child or young person the opportunity to work it out for himself first, then offer lots of praise and reinforcement when he succeeds or makes efforts towards achieving success. If the challenge is too great for him to conquer alone, help him explore the options, knowing that if he chooses one course of action and it is unsuccessful, he will need to persevere and try something else.

As workers and parents/carers, it is so important for us to help children to realise that problems are challenges that can often be solved. If we can help children to break the problem down into its composite parts, we can begin to teach valuable skills that children can apply time and time again in diverse social and learning situations.

There are lots of ways to do this playfully. You could suggest that the child or young person breaks down a seemingly simple everyday task, such as making his bed or a cup of coffee. He could write down or draw each step of the process as a basic set of instructions. You should then follow the instructions literally, without adding any missing steps, no matter how obvious. Encourage the child to comment on your progress; of course any mistakes you make reflect the accuracy of his instructions to you. What can you then learn together about the order in which the process needs to be carried out and the degree of detail required in the description in order to successfully complete the task?

A second option is to play 'Detectives'. Give the child a list or bag full of clues, which are the only things the child will have to help him guess the identity of a mystery person. He has to examine each clue carefully and individually to build a composite picture of who the individual might be. You may need to slow the child down, to stop him from jumping to conclusions before he has examined all the evidence. This is a great quick activity for stressing the need to break problems down into small parts that can be look at individually. For example, if the mystery person was the Queen of England, you could have a list that included:

- crown or tiara
- London bus
- soldier
- Church of England
- corgi dog
- palace.

When children learn problem-solving skills, they gain confidence in their ability to make good choices. One of the key elements in building resilience or 'the qualities which cushion a vulnerable child from the worst effects of adversity…which can help a child or young person cope with, survive and even thrive in the face of great hurt and disadvantage' (Gilligan 1997, p.12) is efficacy. This translates into the child having a sense of effective control over himself and tasks in his life and to having the skills to participate in life, in decision-making and in the future (see Hellett with Simmonds 2003, p.114). Children who are vulnerable by virtue of earlier trauma need to learn that they are no longer powerless and can exert control over many elements of their lives. Helping these children by offering simple choices and developing problem-solving skills is essential in building a sense of their own efficacy:

> All children need to learn how to solve problems and cope with the process of doing so, including inevitable frustration and disappointment. The experience of trauma can make it hard for children to develop good enough problem solving skills that enable them to solve every day problems. Helping a child to plan and rehearse their problem solving skills when they are worried can be extremely helpful. (Hellett with Simmonds 2003, p.116)

Evidently, for many vulnerable children and young people, there is a potential discrepancy between learning the theory of keeping safe and putting it into practice in different settings, with different people at different ages, as possible problems arise. The protective behaviours model teaches problem-solving in a 'one step removed' way in order to avoid scaring children into staying safe, relying, for example, on 'stranger danger' myths, re-traumatising children who have already been victimised or by frightening vulnerable or younger children who haven't had any previous inappropriate sexual encounters (see Gordon 1995, p.75). Children are supported to concentrate on their own feelings and bodily responses using, 'what ifs'; this provides the first protective step. You will not be talking to the child about something that has, will or is happening to him. It is all in the realms of possibility – how could you keep safe, even if…

It is important that we broaden the learning out to diverse situations so that children don't only apply the rules about keeping safe to one situation-specific area. Begin with thinking about fairly everyday possibilities that are adapted to fit the age and gender of the child or young person yet don't conform to gender stereotypes:

- How could someone feel safe *even if* he got lost at a football match?

- How could someone feel safe *even if* he fell and cut his knee at the park?

- What could someone do to keep safe *even if* he had lost his house key on the way home from school and there was no one home to let him in?

- How could someone feel safe *even if* he was at the top of a climbing wall and was too scared to climb back down?

- How could someone feel safe *even if* he heard scary noises when he was in bed at night?

Generate a range of suggestions in order to filter down to get the safest available options. You can then, particularly with older adolescents, broaden the issues to problem-solve in the same one-step removed style around verbal or emotional harm, physical violence and sexual behaviour. For example:

- How could someone feel safe, *even if* someone was shouting at him or calling him names?

- How could someone feel safe in his home, *even if* he was worried someone might try to break in to harm him?

- How could someone feel safe, *even if* someone was touching him in a way that made him feel uncomfortable?

- How could someone feel safe at a party, *even if* he realised he had no money to get a bus/taxi home?

The concept of persistence and assertiveness is vital here. 'Children who are able to stand their ground about what they believe is right and to express their opinions effectively are less likely to be exploited by others. Helping children to "read" situations, choose options and make decisions enables them to be more in control of a situation' (Schonveld and Myko 1999, p.7). There are lots of ways to rehearse this with children and young people or to pre-teach so they are more confident about what to do when they really need to make a good choice about their own safety and to problem-solve.

Remember that not all the strategies you come up with will suit every individual or every situation; the main objective is to support the child or young person to realise he has a number of options.

However, in order to plan your intervention, you need to consider the child or young person's developmental stage (early childhood, middle childhood or adolescence) in order to respond appropriately. First, you need to understand where the child is at, particularly when that child has experienced trauma. 'For many people, the problem solving steps are an unconscious, rapid process used to assess situations and make various choices. For children exposed to trauma, however, these steps are skipped as they move straight to reaction. The goal of this work, then, is to make this unconscious process, *conscious*' (Blaustein and Kinniburgh 2010, p.178; original emphasis).

As executive functions (an umbrella term for the neurologically based skills involving mental control and self-regulation) are still developing into adolescence and young adulthood, it is also important to be realistic, particularly about the capacity for young children to independently problem-solve. The focus in early childhood should be on beginning to understand choice, actions and consequences at a basic level – the 'when...thens'. In middle childhood, you should see an increase in capacity for goal-directed activities – increase your focus on supporting the child to anticipate, plan and evaluate different choices and the possible consequences or outcomes of those choices. In particular, pay lots of attention and praise choices that have had positive or successful outcomes for the child. Lastly, in adolescence, in normal circumstances, the young person should have developed the capacity for more critical, analytical thinking and independent problem-solving. If he has experienced trauma, however, this area is likely to remain a great challenge (Blaustein and Kinniburgh 2010, pp.185–186). Remember that developmental considerations are key to pitching this work at the right level.

This is real life. Children don't always want to engage in your structured activities when you bring them to a session. It is important therefore to recognise that there are many different opportunities in an average day to apply or develop problem-solving skills, which is why it is important to have the parent/carer on board where possible. They can they look for moments when the child might be confused about why something has happened or when he is unaware that something is a problem to someone else. This can really help with teaching an *understanding of both internal and external cues* that signify a problem. To increase *consciousness of choice*, parents/carers should look to explore times when their child identifies a time where he felt he had no choice at all. To improve the child's *understanding of consequences for his actions*, listen for moments when he talks about a negative choice he has made or is planning on making, or notice times where he takes responsibility for a choice he made. This allows for more responsive exploration (Blaustein and Kinniburgh 2010, pp.182–185). These skills are hard to assimilate in ideal practice conditions, so you have to expect that children and young people will need a lot of time and practice to use them in the real world. Repetition is the key, even if it takes a while for the skills to be learned. Over time the aim is that the children will be increasingly aware that they have a choice, even where they are not always able to exercise it in the moment. This is definitely an important step in the right direction.

The activities in this chapter will support children and young people in:

- practising problem-solving, formally and informally
- improving understanding of choice and decision-making
- developing strategies to overcome everyday problems
- encouraging persistence
- differentiating between assertiveness and aggression.

Alternative Simon Says

Materials

None – just a large room.

Process

This activity is best done in groups, so it would be good to use with a family or sibling group. Grotsky *et al.* (2000, pp.263–264) suggested this amendment of the traditional children's game, and I really love it. It's great if you've got a restless or over-active group of children as it gets them up and moving.

Explain you're going to play a new version of the old game 'Simon Says'. In this game, when Simon asks you to do something that you don't want to do, you can say 'no' and you don't have to do it. Otherwise the rules are the same. Pick someone to be 'Simon'. The group must only follow his instructions if he remembers to say 'Simon says' when giving the command. For example, 'Simon says hop on one leg', 'Simon says pull a funny face.' If he doesn't say 'Simon says' and someone follows the command, that person is out. For example, 'Roar like a lion', 'Take three steps backwards.' The last person left is the winner.

Aims

- To build on the child's self-efficacy and sense of control over his safety and choices.

- To build self-protection skills.

- To build assertiveness skills.

Handy hints

Be careful introducing this game if you have children with a strong need to be in control who will only play if they can always be Simon – the next one to lead is usually the winner of the preceding game.

Also be mindful of those children who will be inclined to say 'no' to every command or who are in a particularly oppositional or defiant state of mind. Remember that this is about assertiveness and making positive, active choices, and not about controlling the game.

Self-protection and Soothing

Materials

Pens and paper; you could also use the 'Things that help me feel safe' worksheet (see page 118).

Process

This is an activity I usually use with children aged 5–12, but I see no reason why it couldn't be adapted for older adolescents in thinking about increasing felt safety and decreasing unhealthy coping strategies.

Support the child to identify his own personalised list of things that make him feel safe. Some children will like the containment of a worksheet, while others will prefer to create an image or collage to represent their safe things. You could work with the parent/carer to gather as many of these objects together as possible at home to support the child, or take a photograph of the image for the child to carry with him or to keep at home.

You could also extend this activity to have different smelling items in little pots for the child to sniff, such as perfume, essential oils or toothpaste. You could bring different sounds for them to listen to – music, someone singing, laughter, etc. You could also have various items in a 'feely bag' with different textures for the child to touch – cotton wool, velvet, pine cone, etc. (Link this activity with ideas from the *Sensory Book of Safety* on page 74.)

Aims

- To learn about internal boundaries.

- To build self-protection skills and a healthy body image.

- To increase the child's capacity to define and express his safety needs.

- To encourage the development of self-soothing behaviours and therefore a sense of safety.

Handy hints

You could prepare a 'Things that help me feel safe' worksheet that incorporates some of the following ideas:

The place that helps me feel safe is…

The colour that helps me feel safe is…

The thing that helps me feel safe is…

The person/people that help me feel safe is/are…

The smell that helps me feel safe is…

The food/taste that helps me feel safe is…

The sound/music that helps me feel safe is…

The animal that helps me feel safe is…

Child Safety Plan

Materials

You can either produce a worksheet in advance of the session, or make an image or poster using craft materials, paper and pens to create a personalised *Child Safety Plan*.

Process

In this activity you will help the child to create an individual safety plan. Planning for safety, even if the immediate risk has passed, is important. It should look at the potential risks the child may face, his physical and emotional needs, and also equip him to make positive choices. If you have completed a risk assessment, use this to make the plan relevant to the young person and his current situation. Some children will enjoy creating this from scratch, perhaps in poster form, while others will prefer to complete a worksheet. Whichever method you choose, it should include the following ideas:

THIS IS MY SAFETY PLAN

If I feel scared or unsafe or get my early warning signs, I might not be able stop the feeling straightaway, but this is what I can do to try to keep safe:

1. Find a safe place – this might be inside or outside the house.

2. If it is safe, call the police or my parent/carer. The emergency number is [insert number].

3. I will say:

My name.

What is happening.

Where I am.

4. I could also get help from/talk to [insert name] from my safety network. I can contact him/her at [insert location or telephon number]. If they are not available I should try [insert name].

5. The people that know about my plan are:

Me.

Others [insert names].

You can think with the child about what he would do if he needed help and didn't feel safe. Explore the different scenarios where this might happen. You might need to offer prompts like: 'Would you go to your neighbour's house?' 'Would you call your parents/carers?' 'Would you call the police?' 'Could you find your network person at school?'

Aims

- For the child to develop a practical, workable safety plan.

- To connect the safety plan with work around *Establishing Personal Networks* (see page 64) and *Identifying Early Warning Signs* (on page 44).

- To build on the child's self-efficacy and sense of control over his safety.

- To build self-protection skills.

Handy hints

This can easily be adapted for adolescents who might find themselves in an abusive situation or relationship, where they might not be able or ready to get out of it. For them, you could add a list of people or agencies that will be able to offer support. Think with the young person about how to leave before a situation becomes violent – what are the signs that might indicate that a situation may get out of control or unsafe? How might the young person get around the abuser's attempts to prevent escape? What might the young person keep handy that is ready to go in case of emergency? This could include keys (house or car), money, phone and charger, prescription or any regular medication, and a travel card.

Talking with vulnerable children and young people about what they would do can offer them tremendous strength and resources. It can help them to feel more confident to consciously make safer choices and to protect themselves when they need to; they now have a plan, and this makes them less vulnerable. You might set a task in between sessions following this activity for the child to practise asking for help before you next meet, even if this is just for help in generating possible choices. Teach them that there is always more than one way to solve a problem, even if one of the choices is to do nothing at all. There may be times when the child needs to work on how he feels and/or thinks about a problem first, rather than taking any direct action steps to solve it.

However, it also important to think about assessing real versus perceived danger. There is some psycho-educative work to be done here as children who have been in danger before can get really skilled at reacting quickly when they have thoughts or feelings that seem to signal danger. Sometimes there is real danger, of course, but sometimes the clues are that something has reminded the child of danger from the past; this trigger then activates the body's alarm system. Support the child to pair up his ability to recognise he has an early warning sign (see the *Identifying Early Warning Signs* activity on page 44) with the ability to quickly scan his environment to assess whether he is actually in danger.

There are multiple trigger types: internal (like feeling alone or out of control), relational (intimacy or someone exerting authority) or sensory (a smell, sound, taste, facial expression, touch). Link the 'fight-flight-freeze' response with their personal triggers as different responses may connect with different triggers. You could link up with some of the activities you have done previously around emotional regulation or modulation tools, such as the *Relaxation Techniques* (see page 80), social resources such as a teacher or other safe adult, or visual tools such as a mini 'STOP' sign.

Secrets and Secret Enablers

Materials
Cards with a variety of different secrets: some good/safe/comfortable secrets and some bad/unsafe/uncomfortable secrets (see below for ideas) and felt tip pens.

Process

Explain to the child that while it can sometimes be good fun to keep a secret, it always depends on the kind of secret. There are two different kinds of secrets. Secrets that make you feel good are usually only kept for a short while and when shared, will usually make someone else feel good. Examples of good secrets are a surprise party for a family member or a child winning a school prize. Secrets that make you feel bad may make someone feel unsafe, may need to be kept forever, may not be shared with anyone, or may come accompanied by a threat. If only two people know the secret, it is more likely to be a bad secret. A bad secret might give the child an early warning sign and he should always tell someone on his safety network.

Schonveld and Myko (1999, p.15) have suggested some helpful questions to help children when they're not sure about a secret and can't decide whether to tell a network person about it (see *Establishing Personal Networks*, page 64). I have summarised them here.

QUESTIONS TO HELP DECIDE IF A SECRET MAKES YOU FEEL BAD/UNSAFE OR GOOD/SAFE

- Does this secret give me an early warning sign? (See *Identifying Early Warning Signs*, page 44.)

- Does it mean I will have to do something I don't usually do?

- Is the person sharing the secret someone I trust? Is s/he in my network?

- What might stop me telling this secret?

- Who am I supposed to be keeping this secret from?

QUESTIONS TO ASK ABOUT SECRET PLACES

- If I go to this place, can I get home or leave when I choose?

- Can I get help when I am there, and from whom?

- Does anyone in my family or in my network know where I am?

QUESTIONS TO ASK ABOUT BEING ALONE WITH ADULTS

- Do I trust this person? If so, why?

- Have I been on my own with this person before?

- Do I feel safe with him/her/them?

- Do my parents/carers know I'm with him/her/them? Would they approve?

There are different ways to explore this further. You might prepare a list of secrets on cards and ask the child to choose whether to put them in the 'good/safe secret' pile or the 'bad/unsafe secret' pile. You could prepare the same statements on a worksheet and ask the child to colour the good secrets green and the bad secrets red.

Here are some examples of secrets:

Someone touched your private parts.

You made something for your parent/carer for Christmas at school.

The present you chose for your best friend's birthday party.

Another child in your school is calling you unkind names.

You saw somebody steal something from your local shop.

Someone is regularly taking your school lunch money from you.

The place where your family hides the spare key for emergencies.

Where you keep your treasures.

Your friend is being hit by his dad.

Where you hide your pocket money for safe keeping.

You wet the bed.

You drank some alcohol at a party.

Aims

- To support the child to understand the difference between secrets that make him feel good/safe/comfortable and those that make him feel bad/unsafe/uncomfortable.

- To teach the child he should never keep secrets about touching or experiencing early warning signs, and should always tell a network person if someone asks him to keep a 'bad' secret.

- To teach the child about secret enablers, that is, strategies that perpetrators use to get children to keep a secret. (See below for more on this.)

Handy hints

As you play this game, you will need to explore age-appropriate examples and ways in which perpetrators manipulate children to get them to keep secrets. Think about the following techniques that children have shared:

- Threats: Warnings about what will happen if the child tells the secret, often that the child or someone/something precious to him will be hurt or killed.

- Tricks: The abuse is made into a game or is connected in some sense with love or fun. For example: 'I do this to you because I love you' or 'Let's play the tickling game.'

- Lies: That no one will believe the child if he tells.

- Guilt: That it is the child's fault for 'leading the adult on' or that the child will be responsible for the adult going to prison or getting into trouble if he tells.

- Bribes: Treats, gifts or special treatment if he cooperates and promises not to tell.

- Shame: That if the child tells, everyone will think he is 'bad' or naughty.

Remember that children may hold beliefs and fantasies about abusive situations that might seem utterly illogical to us as adults, yet when we consider children's responses in the context of their developmental age and stage, they can make much more sense. Younger children will naturally hold an egocentric view of the world, and view themselves as responsible for everything that happens, even abuse. Older children, while less egocentric in their thinking, will also be quick at times to generate and justify the reasons why they must be to blame in some way.

Stepping Stones

Materials

Sheets of A4 paper and cut-out stepping stones; felt tip pens.

Process

Ask the young person to draw himself on a piece of A4 paper – this can be as creative or as simple as time and the child allows. Put this on the left hand side. Have the stepping stones in the middle and another blank A4 sheet on the right hand side.

Ask the child to think about how he would like life to be for him in one, two, five or ten years' time – whatever seems most suitable. For some young people, it might need to be much smaller timescales – tomorrow, next week or in three months. This is called a future vision. Prompt a discussion by asking questions depending on individual circumstances, such as:

- Will you be in a relationship? What will your partner be like?

- Will you have a job?

- Will you be safe?

- Will you be in school?

- How will you be feeling?

You can draw this future self or add the details of his life to the blank sheet on the right hand side. Explain that the stepping stones are the steps to achieving these goals. What would the child or young person need to do to get from the present (left-hand box) to the future vision (right-hand box)? There may be different routes across, and it can help to think about a number of alternative pathways to maximise the young person's chances of success. It is about breaking down the steps to make them more achievable and to set the young person up to succeed.

Aims

- To build self-esteem.

- To explore future life visioning – where you would like your life to be at some stage in the future and how you will achieve this.

- To problem-solve – to think about the steps to improving a situation or a relationship or moving forward.

Handy hints

This works better with young people where you have already done some work around building self-esteem and resilience. As part of setting up this activity it is a good idea to use some prompt questions to reconnect with that work.

Preference and Choice

Materials

Scaling number cards from 1–10 (optional).

Process

This activity is best done in a group – it could be a sibling or family group, but could be also adapted for an individual. Ask the group members to choose between two things, and preferably have a range of options in your mind. Examples are:

Day or Night

Strawberries or Blueberries

Football or Tennis

Sunshine or Snow

Home or School

McDonalds or a home-cooked Sunday roast

Playing inside or Playing out

Being alone or Being in a group.

Either imagine a line going across the room, or use scaling number cards from 1 to 10. If the child really loves playing football in the winter and tennis in the summer, he might stand in the middle of the 1:10 scale. If the child is a real home bird and hates school, he might choose to stand at the home end. Children will place themselves at different spots on the line, and this opens up opportunities to have follow-up discussions about the right to make different choices, how some choices are easier to make than others, how some people might feel they should make the same choice as a friend or how it might feel hard to have a different view to everybody else. If appropriate, you could extend this to thinking about choices around safety.

Aims

- To explore the idea of preferences and choices.

- To explore the rights of individuals to make choices and decisions and to respect differences in each other.

Handy hints

Another adaptation suggested by Golding and Todd (1994, p.47) is to ask the child to place himself on a continuum representing really liking something or really disliking something, for example, sweets, homework, going to the seaside.

Chapter 6

Working with Vulnerable Adolescents

Introduction

One of the most important things to stress about this chapter is that if your work is with high-risk or vulnerable adolescents, the activities in the previous chapters of this book are all relevant to you. This chapter definitely does not stand alone, but in it I hope to draw your attention to additional factors to consider in relation to working with teenagers.

Remember that while there is no stereotype for a sex offender or exploiter of young people, they often have a checklist for grooming, and look for or gain access to the adolescent who:

- may not know the difference between right and wrong sexual behaviour
- would be afraid if the abuser threatened him or his family
- feels he can't say no because the abuser is someone he trusts
- will keep a secret
- lacks a sense of affection/attention from parents/carers and can be convinced the abuser loves him
- will be too embarrassed or ashamed to tell his parents/carers
- has a history of difficult or challenging behaviour and may not be believed if he told.

They tend not to target resilient, confident, securely attached children and young people; they target those young people who they feel might already be broken, who wouldn't be believed if they tried to tell, or who wouldn't be deemed credible witnesses in the criminal justice system. Offenders can somehow justify to themselves, in creating their own cognitive distortions to overcome both internal and external inhibitors to offend, that these young people 'don't count'. Your work with these young people should absolutely be about building resilience. It should incorporate work around understanding their bodily responses to stress and danger. It should support developing problem-solving skills and building a sense of safety. This is all vital, protective work.

First, let's acknowledge that adolescence is a time of great challenge and tumultuous change, arising from a complex set of external and internal forces. There are *biological* challenges to cope with in relation to puberty, and these changes lead, in turn, to physiological, sexual and emotional changes. These shifts happen at different ages and different rates, so it is easy for adolescents to quickly feel out of step with their peers. There are also changes to the sleep–wake pattern, with evidence of needing more sleep during puberty, increased daytime sleepiness, and a shift in the circadian rhythm (biological clock) to a preference for later sleep and wake times.

As sexual drives increase, the young person is inevitably faced with additional issues of sexuality and sexual identity that influence decision-making around relationships. During adolescence the sex hormones are especially active in the brain's emotional centre, the limbic system. Not only do feelings reach a flash point more easily, but adolescents also tend to seek out situations where they can allow their emotions and passions to run wild. They are actively looking for experiences to create intense feelings. This thrill-seeking may have evolved to promote exploration, an ability to leave home, become independent and follow one's own path. But in a world where drugs and alcohol, gangs and potentially dangerous relationships beckon, it also puts the teenager at risk (see Wallis and Dell 2004). Although many studies suggest adolescence is the healthiest, most resilient period of the lifespan, overall morbidity and mortality rates increase between 200 and 300 per cent from childhood to late adolescence, and the primary causes for this are related to problems with controlling behaviour and emotions. There is also a link with risk-taking, sensation-seeking and erratic (emotionally influenced) behaviour (see Dahl 2004).

Cognitively changes are also happening as the adolescent brain is blossoming at the same time as his body. There are three crucial pieces of information about the teenage brain that are vital from a safeguarding perspective, but also potentially terrifying for parents/carers. The first relates to novelty – all brains are attracted to novelty, but adolescent brains are dominant in this area, meaning that they crave experience and want to explore and experience anything new. This has terrific implications for academic learning, but also relates to less desirable new behaviours such as experimentation with drinking alcohol, taking drugs and sexual activity. Second, to complicate the matter further, the adolescent brain is attracted to risk-taking behaviour. The resultant chemical response when adolescents are exposed to risk is a very powerful, addictive 'feel good' experience. Third, and crucially:

> between childhood and adulthood, the brain's 'wiring diagram' becomes richer, more complex and more efficient, especially in the brain's frontal lobe…an important part of the frontal lobes is the prefrontal cortex (PFC) which is often referred to as the CEO or executive of the brain and is responsible for such skills as setting priorities, organising plans and ideas, forming strategies, controlling impulses and allocating attention. (Weinberger, Elvevåg and Giedd 2005, p.1)

The critical factor in this is that at the point in their lives that young people are most attracted to novelty and risk-taking, they have not yet developed the capacity to always make good choices and to inhibit inappropriate impulses. Good judgement is something we learn, but only if we have the necessary hardware. If the brain circuitry required for such control is not fully mature in early adolescence, these tasks are rendered so much more difficult, particularly when in the company of other young people.

Psychologically the most important tasks of adolescence are the formation of a personal identity together with individuation, 'whereas a child is joined with parents and family, the adolescent moves away into a separate space becoming a separate individual' (Geldard and

Geldard 2004, p.9). This phase is also characterised by emotional reactivity and high intensity emotional responses often to relatively minor stimuli. There is evidence that adolescents hear information differently to adults. Where adults use their frontal lobe to deduce meaning from verbal and non-verbal communication, adolescents rely on their amygdala, the emotional centre of the brain, and tend to respond more 'from the gut'. They hear a disproportionate amount of negativity, rejection and criticism, and respond on an emotional level to language. They can also struggle to regulate their mood well as this, again, is a function of the pre-frontal cortex where there is major ongoing development during adolescence.

All these changes interact with the *social* challenges of adolescence in terms of fitting in, finding their place in society and in their community. Adolescents can have very changeable personas, and are often willing to experiment with diverse and often contrary psycho-social styles. Parents/carers are replaced as the primary mode of reference for a young person by his peer group, as it is the friendship group who will be perceived to offer unconditional support. Young adolescents spend up to 50 per cent more of their free time out of school with their friends than with parents/carers, as groups of friends begin to expand and close relationships become more intimate (see Brewer 2001, p.247). This is adaptive behaviour; in order to find a position in the social hierarchy, to find a sexual partner and to form alliances and compete with peers, young people need to learn vital social skills. If adolescents were perfectly happy staying at home living with their parents/carers, with no desire to explore the world, the species would soon die out. Acquiring the necessary skills to survive independently requires young people to take risks, seek novelty and venture out of the family home. This, in turn, necessitates a separation from parents/carers and other authority figures – a natural inclination to be in conflict with adults helps adolescents find their own way. 'Transgression now becomes a way of life, as teenagers set out to deliberately distance themselves from adults – often breaking as many adult conventions as they can via their clothes, language and attitudes...most teenagers simply align themselves completely with their peer group' (Brewer 2001, p.248).

There are many hazards in adolescence, not least because they are less dependent on family relationships for protection as they form new relationships and have new experiences. It is a time of experimentation, but this can bring associated risks, as the egocentric adolescent often feels invincible. At a time when taking unnecessary and unsafe risks is the biggest danger to health, adolescents will often see it as exponentially riskier to lose the acceptance of their friends than to physically harm themselves. Geldard and Geldard (2004, p.34) identify the following risk factors: the struggle between peer and parental pressure; peer groups and gangs; smoking, alcohol and drug use; sexual behaviour; risk-taking involving anti-social behaviour (shoplifting, vandalism, driving at high speed, fire lighting); and body weight control as young people are so vulnerable to modelling by others. Just because their bodies are becoming physically mature doesn't mean they are able to appreciate the consequences of behaviour or have the ability to process information in the way adults do.

The risks to young people of becoming victims of child sexual exploitation have become more known to the general population following a number of high-profile investigations in towns and cities across the UK in recent years. This 'is a form of sexual abuse in which a young person is manipulated or forced into taking part in a sexual act. This could be as part of a seemingly consensual relationship, or in return for attention, affection, money, drugs, alcohol or somewhere to stay' (Barnardo's Scotland 2014, p.7). We still have much to learn in this field as we shift the parameters of safeguarding frameworks to include the needs of older children and young people, not least in terms of how to intervene and work directly with young people, wherever possible identifying risk at a much earlier stage, thereby disrupting potential abusers.

Barnardo's has identified three distinct models of abuse that might help us learn about the ways in which perpetrators operate (2014, p.8), to therefore become more aware of how to intervene and to protect vulnerable young people at the earliest opportunity. I have summarised them here:

Inappropriate relationships:

- Usually involves just one abuser who has inappropriate power or control – physical.

- Emotional or financial – over a young person. The young person may believe they have a genuine friendship or loving relationship with their abuser.

Boyfriend:

- The abuser grooms the victim by developing a 'normal' relationship with them, giving them gifts and meeting in cafes or shopping centres. A seemingly consensual relationship develops, but later turns abusive. Victims are required to attend parties and to sleep with multiple men, and threatened with violence if they try to seek help.

Organised exploitation and trafficking:

- Victims are trafficked through criminal networks – often between towns and cities – and forced or coerced into sex with multiple men. They may also be used to recruit new victims. This serious organised activity can involve the buying and selling of young people.

Barnardo's Scotland (2014, pp.15–17) also highlights the risk factors we should all be mindful of, which I have summarised below.[1] They should include, but not be restricted to:

- *Regularly staying out late or repeated missing episodes.* Is the young person missing overnight, or longer?

- *Multiple callers.* Does the young person get a lot of messages or calls from unknown adults or young people who are older than her? Phones are increasingly being used to control victims.

- *Use of mobile phone(s).* Does the young person use her phone excessively? Is she secretive about who she is contacting and why?

- *Expressions of unhappiness.* Is the young person self-harming, showing signs of eating difficulties or challenging behaviour?

- *Disclosure of physical/sexual assault that is later withdrawn,* perhaps indicating a threat to keep quiet.

- *Sexually transmitted infections or a high number of known sexual partners.* The young person may be being forced into having *unsafe sex with multiple people.*

---

1   While I have chosen to use 'she' rather than 'he' in this section, as the research focuses primarily on vulnerable girls, the risks to boys must also be recognised.

- *Non-school attendance or exclusion* increases risk of child sexual exploitation or may be an indicator the young person is becoming involved in child sexual exploitation.

- *Lack of a positive relationship with a trusted adult.* If this is absent, the young person is more likely to seek nurture and attention elsewhere.

- *Drug or alcohol misuse.* Drugs and alcohol are often integral to the grooming process, and may lead to a feeling of acceptance and belonging. The sexual behaviour that then follows can be normalised.

- *Unexplained gifts or money* may be tools of the grooming process.

- *Having an older partner or relationship with a controlling adult, especially where this includes physical or emotional abuse.*

It is important to recognise the warning signs of exploitation in the context of normal adolescent behaviour. Remember that adolescents are relatively inexperienced with dating relationships, and while their relationships may be short-term, they are often experienced as intensely as adult relationships. The combination of a lack of experience and normalisation within the peer group can mean that young people are less likely to recognise or report abusive behaviour towards them (DH 2009, pp.201–202). The research also suggests that adolescents often have differing and sometimes somewhat naive views about definitions of domestic abuse, consent, power and control. They can be more accepting or dismissive of abusive behaviour than adults would be in similar situations. While some young people might welcome support to manage threats to their safety, 'others may aggressively reject support, resisting it for fear of identification, the worry of family shame or "dishonour" or through a lack of recognition of the abuse itself, alongside a desire to exercise choice and agency in decision-making about friends and relationships' (Pearce 2014, p.127). When we take the number of children and young people who are sexually abused by a parent/carer out of the statistics, most sexual victimisation experienced by young women is perpetrated by 'partners' or acquaintances. It can be more difficult for adolescents to report abuse in these situations, particularly when they may not be accustomed to having to advocate for their own safety and wellbeing.

Engaging adolescents in a relationship with a helping adult isn't always the easiest task, particularly when, for most, acceptance within a peer group is paramount; the parts of self they most consciously identify with will generally reflect the current values of their peer group and culture. Yet we know that it is the relationship between the young person and the worker/therapist that is the most important factor in influencing positive change regardless of the model you use to engage the young person (see Prochaska 1999 in Hubble and Duncan 1999). What makes the task more complex still is the concept of the 'secret bind'. Perpetrators will often use drugs, alcohol or gifts to groom young people. They might be invited to places they know they shouldn't go (parties, people's houses they don't know well), and might engage in activities they know they shouldn't be doing (smoking, drinking alcohol or taking drugs). The sex crime will often follow on from these experiences. How much harder it is, then, for young people to tell a safe adult about the sex crime, if they are worried they will get into trouble for being somewhere they shouldn't have been or doing something of which their parent/carer will disapprove.

Disclosure of sexual exploitation is always a challenge for young people; where the grooming processes are incredibly sophisticated, this adds barriers that increase denial. They may worry they'll be labelled 'gay', 'a slag', 'a druggie'. They may feel ashamed or fearful of the response they'll get. Will anyone believe what they're saying if they went with this person willingly? Will there be retribution from the abusers? Conversely, they may not wish the supply of drugs, alcohol or 'love and affection' to dry up. They may not recognise they are being exploited, and even if they do, the perceived disadvantages may be outweighed in the young person's mind by the perceived benefits.

They are also unlikely to talk to someone they don't trust or with whom they don't have a positive relationship. The deep mistrust some adolescents feel towards social workers or therapists may have grown out of negative experiences of previous helping relationships: perhaps their confidentiality was broken, their parents' behaviour didn't change in the way they had hoped, or their situation felt worse as a result of the professional's involvement. These young people may already feel invalidated by and alienated from their parents, teachers and other professionals in their lives; this is particularly the case where young people have been labelled as troublesome, young offenders, sexually mature or promiscuous. We need to look far beyond the presenting behaviours – drug use, sexual activity, aggression or offending behaviour – to ask, what are the drivers? A culture shift is undoubtedly necessary in which all practitioners 'recognise that a child cannot consent to their own exploitation regardless of their external persona, the behaviours they may display or how they come across to other people' (Barnardo's Scotland 2014, p.20). Crowder, with Hawkings, talks specifically about the challenges of engaging adolescent boys who have experienced sexual harm:

> for many adolescent victims, the power of culturally approved mythologies about sexuality and masculinity overwhelms their own experience. Because of this many deny their victimization. They either repress their memories of having been abused, or rewrite their histories and describe their abuse as consensual. Since many offenders are skilful at giving responsibility for their actions to their victims, this misconstruction of reality is generally also supported by the perpetrator. (Crowder with Hawkings 1993, p.126)

Some things might, in time, help the young person to access the right help and support and to let a trusted adult know what is happening to him. It's important to remember that even the most silent, unresponsive adolescents may be weighing us up. We sometimes need to be able to tolerate long silences and still maintain our connection with the young person. By not giving up on the silent or hostile adolescent, we're communicating that we'll stick around until he is ready to talk; we won't give up or give in. You might want to thank him for coming to meet you or for being a good listener, even if you are only together for a matter of minutes. Some young people respond better to trying to make a connection in a non-verbal way: by sharing some of their favourite music (most will have something on their phones), making something creative alongside each other, or taking a walk together. Perhaps in the moment it is about remembering that work with vulnerable adolescents is all about the relationship. You might need to meet for brief sessions over a period of time, before the young person will gradually begin to feel confident in just talking to you and perhaps later in sharing information that will support your work to keep him safe. Above all, we need to be assertive in reaching out to vulnerable adolescents, to make consistent and persistent efforts to set up and maintain contact – in person, by text or on the phone – and to make access to services more adolescent friendly.

Adolescents certainly need a different and perhaps more flexible model of risk prevention and protection than younger children, but just because they are older doesn't mean they are necessarily more robust or resilient; they may have increased experiences of trauma or abuse, which amplify the levels of risk. The adolescent's sense of invincibility often means he is unaware that the circumstances of his childhood leave him vulnerable to abuse. It is important therefore that work with these young people includes the opportunity to develop relationships with a number of different safeguarding adults as part of a multi-agency response to risk management. Key agencies must work together on this. If you're working with this age group, you must be comfortable in doing so. You need to be able to cope with the adolescent's changing moods and rapid attitudinal shifts and challenges without taking on an overtly parental stance or taking offence too quickly. It is challenging work, where rewards are rarely seen quickly.

I often ask the young person what has been tried before – what helped and what didn't – so I can try to avoid making those same mistakes. It is about partnership, 'the need for time to allow the young person to develop trust and confidence and the need for the young person to hold onto some control over their actions' (Pearce 2014, p.138). It's important therefore to establish the young person's goals rather than the system's goals at an early stage. This isn't always easy – you will probably get a lot of 'don't knows' when you try to support young people to establish the goals of your work together, but your chances of effecting positive change will be seriously compromised if you are working to the adult or system's goals rather than the young person's. This is one of the biggest challenges in working with adolescents: how to manage the tension between meeting the parents/carers' needs, expectations and goals and doing the same for the young person. You will need to be a good intergenerational mediator to be able to develop shared goals and, indeed, this might not be possible at first.

This is an area that some in our team have struggled with, and so we have created some very simple laminated cards with suggestions of possible goals from which clients can choose if they are struggling. We have a pack to use with younger children, a pack to use with parents/carers and a pack to use with adolescents. You can edit or tailor the cards to suit the individual.

For risk-taking adolescents, the cards might read:

'I want to self-harm less often.'

'I want to get back into school/education.'

'I want to get along with my parents/carers better.'

'I want to do more activities out of school.'

'I want to stop drinking/using drugs.'

'I want to be in a safe, loving relationship.'

Where young people are not accepting of risk or are not identifying themselves as victims, the process should focus on the here and now and on skill building rather than trauma resolution. Young people will not always cooperate with assessments with as much honesty and detail as you would like; nonetheless, completing a thorough risk matrix in line with your agency's policies and procedures is essential in supporting you to identify areas where you can build on the young person's strengths, successes and positive coping strategies as well as address areas of difficulty or risk. For example, if a young person is not attending school, this would be seen as a risk factor, so the focus initially might be on re-engagement with education or training. If a young person is particularly at risk of going missing straight from school, could he be encouraged to engage in positive adult-led activities late afternoon to re-direct his energy? Your focus must be on the presenting problem or issue that is most pertinent to the young person at the time. Short-term goals work well, and if you can create a series of small successes, this boosts confidence and self-esteem, and increases the likelihood of ongoing engagement. You will find activities in Chapter 5 around the development of problem-solving skills useful in this regard.

You will also have to work hard with parents/carers to support them in managing their child's behaviour and to manage risk, especially where the young person is regularly missing. This includes ensuring they are following relevant protocols and informing the local police. The more time vulnerable children spend away from home, the more vulnerable they become. 'Running away or going missing for periods of time should not be seen as normal teenage behaviour or kids blowing off steam, it should not be assumed they will be okay if they are "streetwise" and will return when they are ready' (Barnardo's Scotland 2014, p.25). We need parents and carers to give an empathic, caring response when young people return from a missing episode, however hard this may be. We want the pull to stay to be stronger than the pull to leave. We also need to understand what is leading them to run away. Key questions such as those suggested below, asked sensitively, and in a timely fashion – probably not when they have just come in through the door, tired and hungry – can help identify whether child sexual exploitation is a factor in the missing episodes.

- *Who have you been with?* Perpetrators often target groups of vulnerable runaways, befriending them by offering gifts and friendship.

- *Where have you been staying?* Perpetrators often offer accommodation as part of the grooming process. Internal trafficking of young people is also an issue; if missing for a few days, the young person may have been taken to other towns and cities.

- *Have you been drinking alcohol or taking drugs?* Perpetrators often lure young people to 'parties' with the promise of drink or drugs, which then facilitates sexual exploitation.

- *Is there a problem that is leading you to run away? What's the root cause?* Often perpetrators exploit pre-existing family problems to further isolate the young person from family members.

Finally, be mindful of personal disclosure and distancing techniques in working with adolescents. Gadd and Hinchliffe (2007, p.10) highlight that it's not uncommon for them to ask personal questions about your sexual experiences, relationships or sexual orientation. There are many different reasons for this. You might be the first adult who has talked to them about sex and relationships. They might see you as a role model who can help them decide the right thing to do. They might be testing your capacity to talk about sexual material. It's important to set yourself clear personal boundaries in relation to this as well as being aware of agency requirements. While there are times when measured self-disclosure can enable an adolescent to feel more comfortable in talking to you, it's also reasonable to expect your personal life to be a private matter, not to be discussed in the workplace. And it's important to remember that the focus must always be on the young person's difficulties, not on your own past or present problems. Most 'young people don't usually want their workers to be their friends or family – they already have those people in their lives. They want professionals they can trust, who are consistent and who demonstrate their positive regard by their manner and professionalism and not by the "secrets" they share' (Gadd and Hinchliffe 2007, p.10). You might want to make sure, if appropriate, that you cover this area in your 'working agreement' (see page 18), which will help to reinforce the boundaries of your relationship.

Wall or Tree of Hope

Materials
Felt tip pens and paper. It is optional to have green card leaves already cut out, or brick shapes/post-it notes.

Process
This is a very simple activity to focus young people on their strengths and goals for the future, to support planning, and to share hopes and dreams. You have two options: one is to make a tree and to have a series of leaf shapes for the young person to write on; the other is to use the idea of building a wall and either drawing a wall made of bricks or having a series of brick-shaped cards on which to write (post-it notes work well for this too).

Work with the young person to build a picture of what he hopes for his future; this could be in the short, medium or long term. He may need prompts with this if he is feeling very stuck or hopeless. For example, 'Where would you like to live?' 'Will you live alone or have a partner or pet?' 'Would you like to be working or studying?' 'Might you travel?' It might be appropriate to include some of your hopes or his parents/carers/teachers' hopes for him. Record each wish or hope on a brick or leaf to build a bigger image.

You might be able to extend this to think about what he needs to do to reach these goals, and link these where appropriate to the idea of making good choices and keeping safe.

Aims

- To explore hopes and dreams for the future.

- To build on resilience and a sense of self-efficacy.

Handy hints

You can also use this technique to explore things the child or young person would like to be better in his life. Try to keep the focus pro-social, as in what he would like to see happen rather than what he wants to stop. For example:

'For my mum and dad to get along' – NOT 'for mum and dad to stop fighting'.

'To concentrate at school' – NOT 'to stop getting detentions'.

'To be in a respectful, safe relationship' – NOT 'to get out of a violent relationship'.

It can be difficult to store larger pieces of work of this nature, so think about taking a photograph; you then have a record of hopes and aspirations to look back on at a future stage.

This activity is a good alternative to *Stepping Stones* on page 125.

Jargon Buster

Materials

A jargon buster sheet or laminated cards with relevant jargon, depending on the young person's previous experiences or current situation.

Process

This activity can be used with groups of young people or individuals. If in a group, there is more scope for discussion and exploration of different understandings, but don't use this as an icebreaker; young people will need to feel comfortable with each other first. Work through the cards or worksheet with the young person, and ask him to explain his understanding of the words. You can then explore definitions or misunderstandings and apply them to different contexts.

Here are some examples in relation to child sexual exploitation:

Partner	Masturbation	Rape
Exploitation	Sex	Kissing
Risk	Confidentiality	Choice
STI	Contraception	Grooming
Love	Consent	Relationship
Safer sex	Trafficking	Homophobia

Aims

- To explore the young person's understanding of the words and their reference to his own life.

- To create a shared understanding and language to move your work forward.

Handy hints

You will need to adapt your jargon to suit the individual circumstances of the young person. You could adapt this to relate to peer-to-peer violence, gangs, self-harm, etc. If you're not sure of some of the definitions yourself, make sure you prepare beforehand, as you only want to intervene if the young person is way off track with his understanding. This is a chance to understand his perspective on a situation as well as creating a shared language. Accept that some subjects are easier to communicate about; you might need to think about how it could be made easier.

Gadd and Hinchliffe (2007, pp.23–24) suggest a group work activity they call 'Body Bits Graffiti'. They label two large pieces of paper 'Male' and 'Female'. They then draw the bottom half of a body on the paper, sometimes, if appropriate, drawing around a seated young person, and create an identity for their man and woman with the young people. The young people are then asked to draw the external sexual and reproductive organs and to label them. Cue lots of laughter and the opportunity to assess whether young people have the correct language for body parts.

Relationships: Me and Other People

Materials

A set of printed cards with the following categories: family, work, friendly, unfriendly, caring, dangerous, trusting, professional, good/close, bad/distant. Small sticky labels or post-it notes.

Process

Explore the word 'relationship' with the young person to try to come up with a shared understanding – relationships are feelings that join us in some way to other people. Those people with whom you have relationships are often people you have a lot of contact with and may be family members, friends or colleagues. Anyone can experience positive and negative relationships; many have good and bad elements at different times.

Spread out the cards ensuring you have a shared understanding of each heading, and ask the young person to write the names of people he knows on sticky labels and attach them to the appropriate cards; it's common for some names to fit on more than one card. For example, a sibling might be a family member but also dangerous at times. This is a way of creating a live visual representation of some of the diverse relationships the young person experiences, and offers the opportunity to explore the nature of relationships in different contexts.

Aims

- To explore different kinds of relationships with young people.

- To explore the complexities of relationships and the ambivalent feelings this can evoke, recognising that relationships can have different components and change over time.

Handy hints

This can be done with individuals or groups, and can be adapted for young people with additional communication needs by using photographs or communication symbols. It can also be adapted for younger children who are struggling to differentiate appropriate boundaries in interpersonal relationships. This might be manifesting, for example, in inappropriate attachments to teaching staff or peers.

Be sensitive to those young people who may be exploring their sexual orientation. Take care, especially in a group setting, to ensure this is managed respectfully in a way that is also appropriate for the context.

This is also a good activity for young people who may have experienced abusive relationships either from within the family group or with romantic partners, to begin to explore appropriate boundaries for relationships.

Self-sabotage

Materials

A 'Sabotage checklist' (see below), paper and felt tip pens.

Process

This activity could also be used with children (from ages nine and older) who sometimes behave in ways that result in them being harmed or unsafe. It can help children notice when they engage in self-destructive or self-defeating behaviours so that they can begin to learn new, healthier strategies for managing in the future.

You will need to create a 'Sabotage checklist' (see below) – it will contain different statements depending on the individual child's age and needs. Work through it with the child or young person and ask him to highlight the three most common behaviours for himself. You might then role-play different scenarios to 'see' the responses in action, but then offer opportunities for different, healthier ways of responding. You can then choose one of the behaviours for the young person to work on over the week, and come up with a plan together of how he will do this. Try to get his parent/carer on board to support, if appropriate.

Aims

- To learn about internal boundaries.

- To build self-esteem and self-efficacy.

- To increase the child's capacity to make conscious, safe choices.

- To build social skills.

- To begin to manage trigger responses, if appropriate.

Handy hints

Ideas for the 'Sabotage checklist' include (adapted from Grotsky *et al.* 2000, pp.237–238):

'I often get headaches, stomach ache or feel sick.'

'I miss school a lot.'

'I don't do my homework.'

'I say unkind things to other people.'

'I don't let people know how I'm feeling.'

'I don't stay friends with people for long.'

'I take drugs or drink alcohol.'

'I feel like I can't fit in.'

'I sleep too much and struggle to get up.'

'I don't sleep enough and I'm always tired.'

'I don't eat properly – I skip meals or eat junk or over eat.'

'I always think it's my fault when something goes wrong.'

'I always blame someone else when something goes wrong.'

'I act like I'm not bothered when I really am.'

'I won't give in or back down.'

'I tell lies.'

'I have sex with people who I don't know or don't like.'

'I have unsafe or unprotected sex.'

'I tease other people.'

'If I'm angry I hit, kick or punch other people or damage property.'

'I run away.'

'I go places with people I have just met.'

'I accept others being violent or verbally abusive towards me.'

'I don't take anything seriously – I'm always acting the clown and making jokes about everything.'

'I accept someone controlling my actions.'

Understanding Emotional Grooming

Materials

This can be a discussion topic, or you can use creative materials to draw or make an image to reinforce the learning.

Process

Although this activity can be done with individuals, it's also good in a group where discussions can develop and themes be explored. First, develop a shared understanding of *emotional grooming* – effectively this occurs when one person manipulates another's emotions to gain control of that person. It's a technique that is often used by people who want to coerce or seduce another into sexual behaviour, and will often be seen in cases of child sexual exploitation or sexual abuse. It can happen at any age, but 'young people who have not developed distinct and healthy personal boundaries are very vulnerable to a groomer's tactics' (McGee and Buddenberg 2003, p.2), as are young people who are yearning for affection or attention.

Even though the target may know something is wrong (see *Identifying Early Warning Signs* on page 44), the groomer often still successfully establishes and maintains a position of power and authority. Explain that learning about the tactics and strategies groomers use will help the young person identify when someone could be trying to manipulate him. Information is power, and enables healthier relationships for all young people. It is important to stress here that a groomer or a target can be someone of either gender. McGee and Buddenberg (2003, pp.8–13) identify two key things that need to be in place for an emotional groomer to successfully gain control of another person: a false sense of trust and secrecy. A target will need to be convinced that the groomer is the only person in the whole world who can be trusted. Work with the young person to think about what might be said or done to support this view, that the groomer should be the most important person in the young person's life. For example:

'I couldn't live without you.'

'You're the first thing I think about when I wake up.'

'It's just you and me against the world.'

'I'll always be there to love and protect you. No one could ever love you more than I do.'

'You know I'd never to do anything to hurt you.'

Other ways of building this trust might be to reassure the young person that the relationship is good, healthy and natural. The groomer will usually begin by taking very good care of the target, buying gifts or protecting him from others. They may treat the young person as a favourite within a group or try to isolate him from his friends or family. Drugs and/or alcohol are often also a factor. They can reduce the target and groomer's inhibitions and impair their capacity to think clearly and logically and to make good, safe choices. They can delay response times and at worse, lead the target to be completely unaware of his environment through passing out. Of course it is also much harder for young people to tell a parent/carer they have been exploited if to tell also involves admitting to drug or alcohol misuse, and groomers know this all too well.

The second area to explore is secrecy. Again, think with the young person about what might be said to maintain secrecy around a relationship. Examples are:

> 'Absolutely no one can know about this. It will ruin what we have.'

> 'I/we'll get into trouble. Do you want that?'

> 'I'll have to move away and then we'll never see each other again.'

You could link this with the activity *Secrets and Secret Enablers* on page 121. It is also worth highlighting here that it is:

> wise to be suspicious of anyone who asks you to keep a secret or hide something from your parents or loved ones, especially if this secret involves a relationship...when you really love someone and they really love you, you want the whole world to know. That's the nature of love – to be shared. (McGee and Buddenberg 2003, p.11)

Other suggestions for statements that might be secret enablers include:

> 'No one would understand our love – we could never explain it.'

> 'Why spoil what we have by letting other people in?'

Or sometimes threats will be preferred:

> 'No one would believe you anyway, if you told.'

> 'If you tell, you'll be sorry.'

> 'You don't want your mum/sister/dog/etc. to get hurt, do you?'

> 'If anyone finds out about us, I'll make sure you regret it for the rest of your life.'

You can either explore these themes in a discussion or create an image or poster that captures the discussion.

Aims

- To ensure the young person understands the process of emotional grooming and to raise awareness of the tactics used by groomers.

- To encourage healthy adolescent relationships.

Handy hints

Think about using role-play to practise the groomer's lines, but also to practise the young person's responses to those lines. Recognise that saying 'no' to someone who is skilled in manipulation through 'language cons' is very difficult. It needs practice. Developing good social communication skills can help young people avoid or resist attempts to coerce or threaten them. Help the young person think of some useful retorts. For example:

'When I said "no", I meant it.'

'I know you don't understand, but you need to respect my feelings.'

'I'm not ready for sex, and I won't be pushed into it.'

'I have too much to lose.'

Normal or Harmful? Resisting Grooming Tactics

Materials

This can be a discussion topic, or you can use creative materials to draw or make an image to reinforce the learning.

Process

Although this activity can be done with individuals, it's also good in a group where discussions can develop and themes can be explored. Alternatively you could co-create a poster presentation or image that explores what McGee and Buddenberg (2003, p.27) refer to as the 'nine grooming tactics' (see below), even though the feelings might be normal in a healthy relationship too. They only become abnormal in the context of manipulation and attempts to control another person.

For each of the tactics – jealousy and possessiveness, insecurity, intimidation, anger, accusations, flattery, status, control and bribery – explore feelings in the context of both 'normal' and 'harmful' relationships. Look at these tactics in the context of potential grooming, and think of ways to notice them and to resist them where possible. Let's work through the first example: jealousy and possessiveness.

Imagine your girlfriend is laughing and chatting to an attractive young man in the dinner queue at the school canteen. It would be normal to perhaps feel a bit jealous and to wonder what they're talking about. There are many ways to manage these feelings. You could wait for the boy outside school that afternoon and beat him up. You could give your girlfriend the cold shoulder and write an offensive post about her on social media. You could act in a way that ensured you girlfriend had no choice but to give you her full attention by threatening to hurt yourself. Or you could 'learn to simply name, claim and tame the feeling' (McGee and Buddenberg 2003, p.27). Tell your girlfriend or a trusted adult how you feel, admit to the jealousy and find a more helpful way to deal with it.

Aims

- To support young people in recognising grooming tactics.

- To encourage healthy adolescent relationships.

- To support young people to develop strategies for managing strong feelings in a more helpful way, which is the key to healthy relationships.

Handy hints

There are many other activities in this book that link well with this. Look particularly at those around emotional literacy, body awareness and boundaries. Young people are far less vulnerable to exploitation and manipulation if they have learned to manage their feelings and can set healthy boundaries for themselves and for others.

Chapter 7

Online Safety

Introduction[1]

The internet is a spectacular resource for children and young people. It enables them to connect, communicate and be creative across diverse devices on a global scale. Technological advances in the arena are so dynamic that parents/carers may find it impossible to keep up. A young person's online life can sometimes have little distinction from his offline life. I try to maintain my own skills and knowledge to keep pace and so enable me to offer advice and protection in managing my own children's online life and experiences, but I won't pretend it's easy, or that I always get it right.

The NSPCC collated data (see Jutte *et al.* 2015) around online harm specifically in relation to cyberbullying, 'sexting' (sharing inappropriate or explicit images online or through mobile devices), viewing harmful content, child abuse images and sexual grooming. This is a new and emerging area of research that tends to focus on children from the ages of eight or nine upwards. Here is a snapshot of the key messages:

- In 2014 the Internet Watch Foundation worked with partners to remove 31,226 URLs of child sexual abuse images worldwide. This is a 137 per cent increase on the previous year.

---

1   This chapter is primarily aimed at parents/carers rather than workers, as it relates to keeping children safe online, although workers can also use it to advise parents/carers.

- In 2015 it became an offence in England, Wales and Northern Ireland for an adult to send a sexual message to a child.

- Reports of sexting in calls to ChildLine have doubled since 2010/11.

- In England in 2013/14 the number of police recorded offences for 'obscene publications' rose by 31 per cent against the previous year.

- Young people aged 12–15 are more than twice as likely to say they have viewed harmful content online compared to children aged 8–11.

Issues that children and young people experience online may vary depending on their age and online activities. However, Childnet International (2013) has grouped potential online risks into four major categories, which I outline here – conduct, content, contact and commercialism.

Conduct

Children need to learn that their online activity can impact themselves and others because of the digital footprint they create on the internet. Each time a young person visits a website, evidence remains of what was accessed; a record of his online activity is stored, and may be made available for others to exploit. Although it's easy to feel anonymous in an online community, in fact, it's imperative to be aware of who can view and then possibly share the information children routinely post online. People should always *think before they post!* As a general rule, personal information must be kept private and never shared with strangers. It is so easy to fall for scams, where people are encouraged to share personal information, which can lead to identity theft.

Children should be encouraged to use a nickname where possible rather than their full name online to protect their personal information and to create strong passwords for all accounts. Although this can make it harder for their friends to identify them, especially when so much communication is through gamer tags or different profile names, it is an important safety measure. Children should also be talked to about the importance of reporting any inappropriate messages or conversations, images or behaviours, and be shown how to do this.

Content

Some online content accessed through social media, online games, blogs and websites is unsuitable for children and young people. Children may also need help to assess this material in terms of reliability and validity; they should know that there can be legal consequences for using or downloading copyrighted material without permission.

As parents/carers, you should familiarise yourself with the age ratings for games and applications (apps) that can help indicate the level and suitability of the content for children of different ages and capabilities. Look at online reviews from other parents, or talk to parents you know to help you make decisions about this too. This is tricky, particularly for younger adolescents, where your child's peers may have access to games you would prefer your child not to play.

Contact

It is important to emphasise the need to apply good judgement in making friends online. People are not always who they say they are, and once you have added them to your account, they may have access to your personal information. Review and monitor the child's friend lists, and insist, if necessary, on some people being removed, however unpopular this might make you. This is a particularly delicate area when popularity is often rated among children and young people by how many 'likes' their posts get on Facebook or how many followers they have on Instagram.

If a child comes to you for support or advice about how to manage online concerns such as cyberbullying, inappropriate content or illegal behaviour, it can be hard to know how to report it. Information about what to do can be found at the UK Safer Internet Centre.[2] The police agency tackling child abuse on the internet is CEOP (Child Exploitation and Online Protection Centre).[3] Their site has a unique facility that allows parents and young people to make reports of actual or even attempted online abuse. CEOP also has some great video resources available to download for free, to share with young people to facilitate conversations about online safety.[4]

---

2   See www.saferinternet.org.uk/need-help
3   See www.ceop.police.uk
4   See www.thinkuknow.co.uk

Commercialism

Privacy and enjoyment online for children can be adversely affected by advertising and marketing, which can also lead to inadvertent spending online – and this can happen so easily, as many parents and carers have found out to their cost, especially when it comes to FIFA points or in app purchases! Teach your child to block pop-ups and spam emails, and turn off in-app purchasing on devices where you can. I have passwords, for example, on the Google Play Store and iTunes, so no purchases can be made until I have input the password first.

What Else Helps?

There will always be 'dark corners' on the internet: cyberbullying; websites promoting self-harm, eating difficulties or suicide; hate communities; pornography; sexual predators; hoaxes; and scams. The challenge for parents/carers is balancing safety with the need for our children to grow into confident and competent adults with a measured view of the world in which we live. We cannot sugar coat reality; it is important to provide opportunities for healthy risk-taking while offering discrete protection.

The most helpful advice I have found in relation to safer internet use is to maintain an open dialogue with your child about his internet usage. Have the computer set up in a high traffic area of the house, if you can, like a family room, where it is visible and can be used openly. Or insist he plays on his tablet downstairs rather than in his bedroom. You can then monitor as you are simply passing through and this will allow you better supervision of your child's online activity. If you're not sure where or how to start talking to your child about online safety, try these openers:

- Ask what your child likes most about the internet and why – what websites or apps are his favourites? What games does he play? Could you have a turn on a game he likes, or play together?

- Ask how he thinks he might stay safe online. Are there any tips he could share with you? Does your child know where to go for help, where to find safety advice, privacy settings and how to report or block services he uses?

- Encourage your child to help you or a less tech-aware friend or neighbour to do something online – a 'good digital deed'.

- Create opportunities to use the internet together – playing games, doing homework research, looking for a recipe or directions for a day out.

The UK Safer Internet Centre site has collated information, materials and resources from across the UK and Europe. They organise high-profile events such as the annual Safer Internet Day, which is well supported by many schools. They have also produced leaflets specifically for foster carers and adoptive parents that are free to download.[5] Children in care and adopted children may be more vulnerable to online exploitation for a number of reasons: because being exploited has been the norm for them, because they don't perceive the behaviour to be exploitative or because they are drawn to the perceived benefits. One of the biggest risks for this group of children is of making unauthorised or unsupervised contact with their birth family, whether or not they are aware of any inherent potential risks. I know from experience that this can have far-reaching and sometimes catastrophic consequences for children, young people and their families.

Childnet International is another non-profit organisation working in partnership with others around the world to help make the internet a safer place for children. Their website hosts online resources for young people, their parents/carers and teachers, as well as key advice on 'hot topics' on a range of e-safety issues.[6] They have produced a free guide in 11 additional languages for parents/carers on supporting children and young people to stay safe online.

While there are limited creative activities I can present here, there are some basic premises we should all be considering in terms of protecting ourselves and our children from potential dangers, where there is the real possibility of strangers gaining a direct link to our homes and our children's lives. Although you cannot rely on filters

---

5   See www.saferinternet.org.uk/advice-and-resources/fostering-adoption
6   See www.childnet.com

alone to keep your child safe online, do think about using *filtering software to block unwanted or inappropriate content and internet parental controls.* The market leading internet providers in the UK all provide their customers with free parental controls that can be activated simply at any time. Video tutorials on how to download and use these controls are available on the UK Safer Internet Centre website.[7] As a general rule, children under ten shouldn't even be using a search engine like Google unsupervised, as even the most innocuous search can result in inappropriate content appearing on your screen. Make sure you know how to switch on the safe search settings or download a child-friendly internet browser.[8]

As for *online gaming,* Childnet's guide contains helpful advice and information on supporting children and young people playing games online.[9] Gaming platforms, communities and chatrooms are often prime targets for online grooming, particularly of young boys. The same site also aims to help parents navigate the positive and creative ways young people are using social media and networking sites, suggesting possible pitfalls and ways to minimise risks.[10]

Social networking refers to access to any website that allows for social interaction between two or more people. Common examples are Facebook, Twitter, Instagram, Tumblr and Pinterest. Used in moderation, these forums can be a great way to socialise, develop stronger social skills and keep in touch with friends and family. However, it is really important to monitor the child or young person's privacy settings; many don't check their account settings, which means they are at increased risk from cyberbullies, sexual predators and stalkers. Negative online experiences on social media sites can sometimes lead to face-to-face confrontations, physical fights and significant issues with peer relationships.

Cyberbullies use technology to tease, threaten, humiliate or harass another person, through emails, chatrooms, text or instant messages, Snapchat and social media. It is so hard for young people

---

7   See   www.saferinternet.org.uk/advice-and-resources/parents-and-carers/parental-controls

8   Examples of child-friendly internet browsers include ww1.kidzui.com (ages 3–12), zoodles.com (ages 3–13), kid-surf.com (ages 3–8), Kidoz.net (ages 2–8), and www.safesearch.com

9   See www.childnet.com/ufiles/online-gaming.pdf

10   See www.childnet.com/resources/young-people-and-social-networking-sites

to seek refuge from this form of abuse – cyberbullying can happen 24 hours a day, every day of the year. This is sometimes connected with 'trolling', often in chatrooms and on message boards, where people can take advantage of online anonymity. If your child is a victim of cyberbullying, save and document all online texts, messages, videos, etc. and inform the police. This is more difficult if the bully is using Snapchat, an application that lets users control the amount of time the image/video they send can be viewed for (from 1 to 10 seconds) once opened. The idea is that when the recipient opens the 'snap' to see it, it is then hidden and deleted, so it is hard to save evidence of bullying behaviour, unless you are quick enough to take a screenshot. If the abuse occurs on a social media site, you should report the incident using that platform's formal process; the site should then investigate and take action where appropriate.

One of the greatest risks for vulnerable children in particular is seeking acceptance from peers on these sites, especially when friendships in the 'real world' can be such a struggle. As they grow up, these children may spend a lot of time alone, because they are unable either to make or sustain friendships. One of the legacies of emotionally unresponsive parenting is that 'the parts of the child's social brain that are key to the art of making and developing friendships can remain underdeveloped' (Sunderland 2006, p.228). For this child, Sunderland identifies three key areas of difficulty, summarised thus:

- His timing is off: He might interrupt, there can be difficulties with the to and fro of reciprocal communication.

- He struggles to listen to the other child: He might struggle to pick up on social and non-verbal cues. He could have inappropriate body language and stand too close, for example.

- He might not be able to tune in to or interpret the other child's emotional state: He doesn't notice when that child is upset, excited or bored.

Young people can therefore become so intensely focused on their online world that they feel they only have an identity within it. Self-esteem and self-worth can become defined by the number of 'likes' on a photo posted. Some users will post absolutely everything and anything about day-to-day happenings; by posting so much personal information, the risk of potential danger increases. Make sure your child is aware of this.

There is also the potential for peer pressure in relation to sexting, a fairly new phenomenon, which refers to sending sexually explicit or suggestive messages, photographs or videos, usually from one smart phone to another. It may be new, but it is becoming all too common among adolescents. It is considered by some young people as modern-day, harmless 'flirting'. Others do it because they think it will raise their social status. Some will sext in order to hurt or humiliate another person. Of course, once the message is sent, there is no going back. It can be sent from friend to friend to friend, or posted publically online and then sent from stranger to stranger to stranger. It is almost impossible to erase that information from the digital cloud. Where messages intended for one individual are then distributed to others, this can inevitably have a damaging impact on self-esteem and on peer relationships. There are also legal implications in relation to the making, possession and distribution of sexual images of children, even if the people involved are children themselves. There are some good resources that may help navigate this area.[11]

So if your child wants to set up a social media account, do it together and have an open dialogue about the positives and potential pitfalls such as cyberbullying, sexting or information sharing. Most sites don't permit children under 13 to open an account, but it is by no means actively enforced. Make sure you have access to the child's passwords to ensure his safety isn't threatened by outside sources. If you become a friend of the child on the account, this also better allows you to track who he is communicating with – be sure that he is only 'friends' with people he actually knows in real life. Make sure you know how to block any individual with whom you do not want your child to have online contact. For potential sexual predators,

---

11 A leaflet aimed at young people who have posted or sent sexual images can be downloaded at: http://swgfl.org.uk/products-services/esafety/resources/So-You-Got-Naked-Online/Content/Sexting-Toolkit. The Association of Child Police Officers guidelines on sexting can be found at http://ceop.police.uk/Documents/ceopdocs/externaldocs/ACPO_Lead_position_on_Self_Taken_Images.pdf

See also 'A Parent's Guide to Dealing with Sexting': www.saferinternet.org.uk/ufiles/A-Parents-Guide-to-Dealing-With-Sexting-26SEP13.pdf and a short video from the NSPCC on how to stay safe online: 'I saw your willy: Be share aware': www.youtube.com/user/nspcc

building a relationship with a child online can take weeks or even months, while the child is lulled into a false sense of security until he trusts his new friend. This is much less likely to happen if a safe adult closely monitors the child's online activity.

It's also worth drawing attention to research by the University of London reported by *The Huffington Post* (Packham 2015) around how the use of social media and mobile messaging is affecting the English language. This suggested that 90 per cent of UK parents struggle to interpret their adolescent's online communication. 'Fleek' came out as the winner, with 43 per cent of parents unaware it meant 'looking good'. 'Bae', which is often heard in my home, a term of affection meaning 'before anyone else', was also in the top three. There are lots of online guides to these abbreviations and they change very frequently, so I have decided not to reproduce them here. Just don't get left behind.

As a final note, when you are considering what age to give your vulnerable child access to a computer or online device, including a smartphone, weigh up the risks first. Would you leave this child alone in a big city with no adult supervision? Would he have the skills to successfully navigate the dangers and hazards that might beset him? Would he be able to identify potential scams or hoaxes? Would he share any worries he had with you? If not, he might not be ready for total online freedom. I have a rule in my home that I will check my children's tablets and mobile phones on a regular basis; it is a condition to owning them. I check comments and images posted on social media and I check the browser history. It's not a failsafe strategy, but even in the face of accusations of 'spying', I do it to increase the likelihood that their privacy, safety and security are protected. Phones and tablets also come out of bedrooms before bedtime and are switched off.

It's also important to think about how we act as role models for our children in relation to the internet. Whatever you do online – listen to music, download films to watch or browse on Facebook – your child will be watching, learning and potentially wanting to do the same.

Five SMART Rules for Primary-aged Children

Materials

Paper and felt tip pens and collage materials.

Process

Make an acrostic poem based on SMART rules for primary-aged children around internet safety.[12] You might like to display the guidelines where your child accesses the internet, preferably in a family space rather than the child's bedroom.

SAFE

Keep safe by being careful not to give out personal information when you are posting or chatting online. This includes your email and home address, full name, phone number, the school you attend, your age and your password. This is accepted as the riskiest thing you can do online.

MEET

It can be very dangerous to meet someone you have only got to know online. Only do this if you have talked to your parents/carers about this beforehand, and preferably if a trusted adult comes with you. Remember that online friends are still strangers even if you have been chatting online with them for a long time. Sexual predators operate online by gaining children's confidence, collecting their personal details and often pretend initially to be a child or young person themselves. The internet appears to offer such a high level of anonymity that predators can contact potential victims from the comfort of their own homes with much less chance of being traced than would be the case offline. It is so easy to create an alternative identity and to change gender, age and interests to share commonalities with a potential target.

ACCEPTING

If you accept emails or messages or open files or images from people you don't know or trust, this can lead to problems – they may contain nasty messages or viruses that will damage your device.

---

12   These are adapted from www.childnet.com

RELIABLE

You cannot always trust information on the internet, and people don't always tell the truth about themselves. Always check information on other websites, in reference books or encyclopaedias or with an adult you trust. If you really like to chat online, make sure it's with friends or family you know well in the real world. One of the most common forms of cyberbullying involves 'fake' relationships being forged with the intended victim in order to then publically disclose their personal information.

TELL

If anything you experience online helps you feel uncomfortable or scared or worried – for yourself or someone else – tell a parent, carer or trusted adult on your safety network (see *Establishing Personal Networks* on page 64) as soon as you can.

Aims

- To help the child know how to stay safe online.

- To maintain lines of communication in relation to cybersafety between adults and children.

Handy hints
Adapt this for adolescents with these 'Five Tips for Teens'.[13]

- Protect your online reputation and manage your digital footprint by thinking twice before you post. Any content you post online can last forever and could be shared publicly by anyone.

- Know where to find help either through your service provider or by learning how to use blocking and deleting tools. It's never too late to tell someone in your safety network if you have been upset by something online.

- Don't give in to pressure, as once you've pressed send, you can't take it back. Don't lose control.

---

13 Adapted from www.childnet.com

- Respect the law by only using reliable services to legally access TV, music and film online.

- Acknowledge your sources by giving credit when using other people's ideas or work that you have found online. Don't try to pass it off as your own.

Family Internet Agreement

Materials

Felt tip pens and paper.

Process

A good way to set boundaries around internet use in the family is to reach an agreement about what the child can and cannot do online. Talk to your child about what he thinks should be part of the agreement and co-create the document together. Use the 'Five SMART Rules' or 'Five Tips for Teens' (on pages 160–161) as a prompt if needed.

Here are some ideas of areas around which you might like to negotiate:

- Limits on the amount of time spent online or gaming and the time of day (e.g. turning screens off an hour before bedtime).

- Regular screen breaks – at least 5 minutes every 45–60 minutes.

- Not sharing any images or comments he wouldn't be happy sharing with you – link this with exploration of cyberbullying.

- Age restrictions on certain sites.

- Not opening an email unless it's from a trusted person.

- Not giving out personal information – such as phone number, address, school, date of birth, sports team he plays for – to people he doesn't know in real life that could be used to identify or locate him.

- Coming to a trusted adult in his network with any worries about online activity or if he comes across something online that gives him an early warning sign (see *Identifying Early Warning Signs* on page 44 and *Establishing Personal Networks* on page 64).

- The agreement applies whenever the internet is accessed on any device – including at school, at friends' houses or in internet cafes.

- For children in care and adopted children, you might need to consider adding a rule about birth family contact.

Remember that if you are agreeing shared rules, you also need to talk about what the consequences will be if the rules are broken. This might be loss of the online device for a period of time, or increased restrictions on the length of time the young person can use it per day.

Aims

- To reach a shared agreement about internet usage.

- To reinforce messages around cybersafety.

- To create the space for open dialogue with the child/young person.

Handy hints

There are many stories and online resources and video clips you can watch with your child to begin helpful conversations about online risks and what to do about them. There are examples of e-books for younger children, such as *Digiduck's Big Decision*.[14] This is a story of friendship and online responsibility. You might also like *The Adventures of Smartie the Penguin*.[15]

Age-appropriate video clips can also be found by searching on the CEOP website or on the CBBC website where there is also an internet safety quiz.[16]

---

14 This is downloadable as a PDF at www.kidsmart.org.uk/teachers/ks1/digiduck. aspx
15 This is also downloadable as a PDF at www.kidsmart.org.uk/teachers/KS1/ readsmartie.aspx
16 See www.bbc.co.uk/cbbc/quizzes/keep-dodge-safe-online

You might also want to take a look at Hector's World™, which is a series of six cartoons where you can watch Hector and his friends learning to use their computer safely.[17]

Virtual Relationships

Materials
Felt tip pens and paper.

Process
This is not so much an activity as recognition of the need to raise awareness of the dangers of virtual relationships, particularly for our most vulnerable children and young people, for whom relationships in real life might be complicated, unsafe or feel impossible to manage. Email, chatrooms, online gaming, instant messaging through various social media platforms – in recent years these have changed the way we communicate beyond all recognition, bringing individuals and groups of people together through shared interests from all over the world. It is therefore vital that we teach children the differences between relationships in a virtual world and our everyday reality, which is perhaps why it is so attractive (and so risky) to children and young people without the social skills to meet and 'talk' to peers face-to-face. When 70 per cent of communication is said to be non-verbal, there is an inherent risk in online relationships where we cannot learn about people through their body language, social cues or facial expressions (see McGee and Buddenberg 2003, p.67). This significantly impacts on what we understand about the person we are meeting, relating and communicating with.

You could create a poster or image to encapsulate the rules or safe boundaries in terms of relationships and boundaries on the internet. The reality is that practically everyone you 'meet' online is a stranger, so you should apply the usual boundary rules for strangers, even though, after chatting online for days or weeks, you might feel you are becoming friends:

---

17 See www.thinkuknow.co.uk/5_7/hectorsworld

- Never share personal or identifiable information (date of birth, address, school, etc.) on the internet.

- Don't chat with, message or email someone you have not met in real life.

- Avoid all conversations with sexual or illegal content.

Don't forget that the internet offers those with malicious intent an anonymous environment, with unlimited boundaries and easy access to vulnerable people.

Aims

- To reach a shared agreement about internet usage.

- To reinforce messages around cybersafety.

- To create the space for open dialogue with the child/young person around virtual and real life worlds and relationships.

Handy hints

Use this alongside *Relationships: Me and other People* on page 143.

Help and Support

UK

ChildLine is a private and confidential service for children and young people up to the age of 19 providing phone and website advice.
www.childline.org

The Hideout is a website for children and young people with interactive resources to help them understand domestic abuse and where to get help from.
www.thehideout.org.uk

Respect not Fear is a website for young people about relationships and interactive games. There's also a free iPhone app.
www.respectnotfear.co.uk

The Marie Collins Foundation helps children and young people who have been harmed online.
www.mariecollinsfoundation.org.uk

The Child Exploitation and Online Protection Centre (CEOP) helps children stay safe online. If someone has acted inappropriately, it can be reported using an online form. There are also lots of child-friendly resources and videos to support keeping safe.
www.ceop.police.uk

Provision of Therapy for Child Witnesses Prior to a Criminal Trial: Practice Guidance, from the Crown Prosecution Service.
www.cps.gov.uk/publications/prosecution/therapychild.html

Families Feeling Safe is an organisation that believes everyone has the right to feel safe in their community, working with parents and children and the professionals who work with them. They have free downloadable worksheets on their website.
www.familiesfeelingsafe.co.uk

Protective Behaviours Consortium CIC is the national organisation for protective behaviours in the UK.
www.protectivebehavioursconsortium.co.uk

The Protective Behaviours Training Partnership exists to promote the protective behaviours process and to ensure training is of a high standard.
www.protectivebehaviourstraining.co.uk

Protective Behaviours (PB) People is a free community website developed by a group of volunteers whose purpose is to promote the protective behaviours process. There is an online forum to share ideas and resources.
www.pbpeople.org.uk

Dot Com Children's Foundation is a programme built on the core processes of protective behaviours. It aims to empower children to practise positive values and make safer choices in life.
www.dotcomcf.org

USA and Canada

The Canadian Centre for Child Protection aims to reduce the numbers of missing and sexually exploited children and to educate the public around child personal safety and sexual exploitation. They have many 'Kids in the Know Kits' aimed at teaching staff to buy, as well as free and downloadable resources.
www.protectchildren.ca

The Canadian Child Welfare Research Portal provides access to up-to-date research on Canadian child welfare programmes and policies.
www.cwrp.ca

Stopbullying.gov relates to all forms of bullying including cyberbullying, and has some great video links for children to animated webisodes dealing with bullying at school.
www.stopbullying.gov

Usa.gov also has it's own YouTube channel where young people can watch videos around cybersafety and bullying.
https://kids.usa.gov/index.shtml

The Child Welfare Information Gateway connects child welfare and related professionals to comprehensive resources to help protect children and strengthen families.
www.childwelfare.gov

Childhelp has launched a 'Speak up, Be Safe' prevention programme for children in the US that aims to support children and teens learn the skills to prevent or interrupt cycles of neglect.
www.childhelp.org

BeAKid'sHero has free parent tools, videos and resources.
www.beakidshero.com

Australia

Protective Behaviours Australia Inc. aims to enhance the personal safety of children and young people through the use of the protective behaviours programme across Australia, and has links to various regional websites (see the example below for New South Wales). You can order posters through the website.
www.pbaustralia.com

Protective Behaviours Consultancy Group of NSW is a not-for-profit organisation whose primary objective is to reduce the abuse of children and young people in the community. They have a number of resources available to buy online including theme posters, booklets, DVDs and books, together with free downloadable resources.
www.protective-behaviours.org.au

Safe4Kids is a Western Australian organisation that specialises in child protection programmes, specifically designed to combat child abuse by providing children with clear messages regarding inappropriate behaviour.
www.protectingkids.com.au

Kids Matter promotes a mental health and wellbeing framework for primary schools in Australia.
www.kidsmatter.edu.au

Child Wise is one of Australia's leading not-for-profit child abuse prevention organisations, working to build awareness, deliver education and provide tools to empower individuals and communities around Australia to prevent child abuse and exploitation. They have some interesting downloadable publications available through their website.

www.childwise.org.au

See the Australian Law Reform Commission for information on helping a child be a witness in court.

www.alrc.gov.au/publications/14-childrens-evidence/child-witness-courtroom

Recommended Books for Children

Alimonte, F. and Tedesco, A. (2003) *Not Everyone is Nice: Helping Children Learn Caution with Strangers.* Liberty Corner, NJ: New Horizon Press Publishers Inc.
The authors provide a list of guidelines to show children how to protect themselves and how to seek help in frightening situations.

Bodsworth, N. (1991) *A Nice Walk in the Jungle.* New York: Picture Puffin.
This is good resource for reinforcing the idea of persistence in seeking help – you need to just keep telling, which is a vital protective behaviours message.

Brukner, L. (2015) *How to be a Superhero Called Self-Control.* London: Jessica Kingsley Publishers.
Narrated by a superhero called 'Self-Control', this book provides a variety of super power strategies to help children with emotional and sensory regulation difficulties to master control (suitable for ages 4–7).

Giles, S. (2012) *The Children's Book of Keeping Safe.* Worksop: Award Publications Ltd.
This looks at safety issues in broader terms covering areas such as playing safely, safe surfing, safety at home, stranger danger and road safety.

Goodheart, P. (2004) *You Choose.* London: Corgi Childrens.
This book will link well with work around preference and choice and self-efficacy. Aimed at children under seven, it asks that you imagine you could go anywhere, with anyone, and do anything. Where would you live? Who would be with you? What would you play?

Holmes, M. (2000) *A Terrible Thing Happened*. Washington, DC: Magination Press.
This is very gently told story for children who may have witnessed violence or trauma. A little badger sees something that scares and upsets him and he just doesn't know what to do. He's helped to learn that talking to someone can help him feel safe again.

King, K. (2008) *I Said No! A Kid-To-Kid Guide to Keeping your Private Parts Private*. Weaverville, CA: Boulden Publishing.
This book is written from a child's perspective, using a simple, direct approach to body safety including: what's appropriate and with whom, how to deal with inappropriate bribes/treats, when and where to go for help.

Kleaven, S. (1998) *The Right Touch: Read Aloud Story to Help Prevent Child Sex Abuse*. Kirkland, WA: Illumination Arts Inc.
This story offers a gentle educative tool; it's about Jimmy and his mum as she tries to support him to protect himself from sexual harm.

Law, D. (2016) *Secret, Secret*. London: Jessica Kingsley Publishers.
A book to support children to recognise different kinds of secrets – some to keep, some to tell, some to yell.

Moore-Malinos, J. (2005) *Do You Have a Secret?* Durban, Ireland: Clearway Logistics Phase 1a.
This is a book to help with exploring 'good' and 'bad' secrets, and encourages children to talk about it.

Morrisroe, R. (2013) *No Secrets Between Us*. USA: RoeZ.
This story covers all the essentials in terms of keeping safe, while telling the story of a little girl who is sexually abused when she visits a friend. Ideal for three- to seven-year-olds.

O'Malley, J. (2002) *Jasmine's Butterflies*. Australia: Justine O'Malley.
A good resource to link with early warning signs as it tells the story of Jasmine's school trip to the zoo, where she gets lost and feels unsafe. The butterflies in her tummy (early warning signs) mean that she knows she needs to get help.

Power, K. and Power, R. (2014) *My Underpants Rule.* Teddington: Kidsrule Publishing Ltd.
Suitable for children aged 3–8, this book aims to empower children to manage difficult situations and helps reinforce 'The underpant rule' using rhymes and different scenarios.

Saltz, G. (2008) *Amazing You! Getting Smart about Your Private Parts.* New York: Penguin.
This book presents clear and age-appropriate information about reproduction, birth and the differences between girls and boys bodies.

Sanders, J. (2011) *Some Secrets Should Never be Kept.* Victoria, Australia: UpLoad Publishing Pty Ltd.
This book deals with the subject of child sexual abuse through the character of a brave little knight and focuses on grooming techniques. Messages about keeping your body safe are threaded throughout. See *www.somesecrets.info*

Sanders, J. (2015) *No Means No!* Victoria, Australia: UpLoad Publishing Pty Ltd.
This is written from a child's perspective, and using a direct approach covers how to support children to rehearse and remember appropriate responses to keep them safe.

Seeney, J. (2012) *A Safe Place for Rufus.* London: BAAF.
This is a great resource to link with work around feeling safe within your body, as Rufus discovers the power of his safe blue cushion. There are parents/worker notes at the back to give guidance to those who might be worrying about 'getting it right'.

Spelman, C. (2006) *Your Body Belongs to You.* Park Ridge, IL: Albert Whitman & Company.
This helps to explain to children what to say and do if someone touches their body when they don't want to be touched, especially on their private parts.

Smith, A. (2011) *Koala and Bunny: Instilling Protective Behaviours in Children*. Australia: Eloquent Books.
This book aims to help children become more aware of the special parts of their bodies – it is not aimed so much at children who have already been harmed.

Wallis, J. (2014) *Chicken Clicking*. London: Andersen Press.
This is a great little rhyming story to introduce young children to safety on the internet, and is a play on the traditional fairy tale *Chicken Licken*.

Zuckerberg, R. (2013) *Dot*. London: Picture Corgi.
This book is aimed at the over-threes and follows a little girl called Dot who is very skilled at using technological devices, but has forgotten how to live in the real rather than online world.

References

APS (Association for Psychological Science) (2013) 'Teen's brains are more sensitive to rewarding feedback from peers.' 17 April. Available at www.psychologicalscience.org/index.php/news/releases/teens-brains-are-more-sensitive-to-rewarding-feedback-from-peers.html, accessed on 3 March 2016.

Atkinson, C. and Truan, D. (no date) *Protecting Children from Sexual Abuse in the Community. A Guide for Parents and Carers.* London: NSPCC.

Barnardo's (no date) 'All About Me' game. Available at www.barnardos.org.uk/what_we_do/policy_research_unit/research_and_publications/all-about-me-game/publication-view.jsp?pid=PUB-1147, accessed on 3 March 2016.

Barnardo's Scotland (2014) *Guidance on Child Sexual Exploitation. A Practitioners' Resource Pack.* February. Edinburgh: Barnardo's Scotland.

Blaustein, M. and Kinniburgh, K. (2010) *Treating Traumatic Stress in Children and Adolescents. How to Foster Resilience through Attachment, Self-regulation and Competency.* New York: The Guilford Press.

Bomber, L.M. (2011) *What About Me? Inclusive Strategies to Support Pupils with Attachment Difficulties Make it through the School Day.* Duffield: Worth Publishing.

Booth, P.B. and Jernberg, A.M. (2010) *Theraplay: Helping Parents and Children Build Better Relationships through Attachment-Based Play* (3rd edn). San Francisco, CA: Wiley & Sons.

Brewer, S. (2001) *A Child's World, A Unique Insight into How Children Think.* London: Headline Book Publishing.

Brohl, K. (1996) *Working with Traumatized Children. A Handbook for Healing.* Washington, DC: CWLA Press.

Carle, E. (2013) *The Very Hungry Caterpillar Touch and Feel Playbook.* London: Puffin.

Cavanagh Johnson, T. (1998a) *Treatment Exercises for Child Abuse Victims and Children with Sexual Behaviour Problems.* Dover: Smallwood Publishing.

Cavanagh Johnson, T. (1998b) *Helping Children with Sexual Behavior Problems. A Guidebook for Parents and Substitute Caregivers.* Dover: Smallwood Publishing.

Childhelp (no date) Statistics available at www.childhelp.org/child-abuse-statistics, accessed on 13 February 2016.

Childnet International (2013) 'Childnet International response on Culture, Media and Sport Committee Inquiry on Online Safety.' Available at www.childnet.com/ufiles/Childnet-International-response-to-CMS-inquiry-on-Online-Safety---August-2013.pdf, accessed on 24 January 2016.

Cicchetti, D., Rogosch, F., Lynch, M. and Holt, K.D. (1993) 'Resilience in maltreated children: Processes leading to adaptive outcome.' *Development and Psychopathology 5*, 4, 629–647.

Crowder, A. with Hawkings, R. (1993) *Opening the Door: A Treatment Model for Therapy with Boys, Adolescent and Adult Survivors of Sexual Abuse.* New York: Brunner/Mazel.

Dahl, R.E. (2004) *Adolescent Brain Development: A Framework for Understanding Unique Vulnerabilities and Opportunities.* Pittsburgh, PA: University of Pittsburgh Medical Center. Available at www.bluestemcenter.com/articles/Adolescent%20 Brain%20Development.pdf, accessed on 1 January 2016.

Dawson, A. (no date) *The Right to Feel Safe.* Thames Valley Police.

DH (Department of Health) (2009) *Improving Safety, Reducing Harm. Children, Young People and Domestic Violence. A Practical Toolkit for Front-line Practitioners.* London: DH.

Fennell, M. (2009) *Overcoming Low Self Esteem: A Self-help Guide Using Cognitive Behavioral Techniques.* London: Robinson.

Gadd, M. and Hinchliffe, J. (2007) *Jiwsi: A Pick 'n' Mix of Sex and Relationships Education Activities.* London: fpa.

Geisler, D. (2014) *My Body Belongs to Me from my Head to my Toes.* New York: Skyhorse Publishing.

Geldard, K. and Geldard, D. (2004) *Counselling Adolescents (2nd edn).* London: Sage Publications.

Gilligan, R. (1997) 'Beyond permanence? The importance of resilience in child placement practice and planning.' *Adoption and Fostering Journal 21*, 1.

Golding, C. and Todd, F. (1994) *Protective Behaviours Through Drama.* Adelaide, SA: Department for Education and Children's Services.

Gordon, S. (ed.) (1995) *The Right to Feel Safe.* Adelaide, SA: Protective Behaviours Inc.

Grotsky, L., Camerer, C. and Damiano, L. (2000) *Group Work with Sexually Abused Children. A Practitioner's Guide.* Thousand Oaks, CA: Sage Publications.

Hargreaves, R. (2007) *Mr Jelly.* London: Penguin Books.

Harris, R.H. (2004) *Let's Talk About Where Babies Come From.* London: Walker Books.

Harris, R.H. (2008) *It's Not the Stork: A Book about Girls, Boys, Babies, Bodies, Families and Friends.* Cambridge, MA: Candlewick Press.

Hellett, J. with Simmonds, J. (2003) *Parenting a Child Who Has Been Sexually Abused.* London: BAAF.

How, S. (2013) *Tell Me About Your Greatness!* Fargo, ND: How 2 Creative Services.

Jutte, S. *et al.* (2015) *How Safe Are Our Children? The Most Comprehensive Overview of Child Protection in the UK.* London: NSPCC.

Kehoe, P. (1988) *Helping Abused Children.* Seattle, WA: Parenting Press, Inc.

Lippett, I. (1990) *Trust your Feelings. A Protective Behaviours Resource Manual for Primary School Teachers.* Adelaide, SA: Mission Australia Prevention Programs.

Martin, H.-A. (2007) *The Parent's Helping Handbook. A Practical Guide for Teaching Your Child Protective Behaviours.* Armadale, WA: Safe4Kids Pty Ltd.

McElvaney, R. (2016) *Helping Children Tell About Sexual Abuse.* London: Jessica Kingsley Publishers.

McGee, K.M. and Buddenberg, L.J. (2003) 'Unmasking Sexual Con Games.' In K.M. McGee and L.J. Buddenberg (eds) *Unmasking Sexual Con Games: A Teen's Guide to Avoiding Emotional Grooming and Dating Violence* (3rd edn). Boys Town, NE: Boys Town Press.

National Scientific Council on the Developing Child (2015) *Supportive Relationships and Active Skill-Building Strengthen the Foundations of Resilience.* Working Paper 13. Cambridge, MA: Center on the Developing Child, Harvard University.

Nowicki, S. and Marshall, P.D. (1992) *Helping the Child Who Doesn't Fit In.* Atlanta, GA: Peachtree Publishers Ltd.

NSPCC (no date) 'The underwear rule.' Available at www.nspcc.org.uk/preventing-abuse/keeping-children-safe/underwear-rule, accessed on 28 February 2015.

NSPCC (1997) *Turning Points. A Resource Pack for Communicating with Children. Module 5, Practical Approaches.* London: NSPCC.

O'Neill, C. (1993) *Relax.* Swindon: Child's Play International Ltd.

Packham, A. (2015) 'What do Fleek, Bae and FOMO mean? 90% of parents baffled by text speak.' *The Huffington Post,* 1 May.

Pallett, C., Simmonds, J. and Warman, A. (2010) *Supporting Children's Learning – A Training Programme for Foster Carers.* London: BAAF.

Pearce, J. (2014) 'Moving on with Munro: Child Sexual Exploitation within a Child Protection Framework.' In M. Blyth (ed.) *Moving on from Munro: Improving Children's Services* (pp.125–142). Bristol: Policy Press.

Prochaska, J.O. (1999) 'How do People Change, and How Can We Change to Help Many More People?' In M. Hubble, B. Duncan and S. Miller (eds) *Heart and Soul of Change: What Works in Therapy.* Washington, DC: American Psychological Society.

Protective Behaviours Consultancy Group of NSW (no date) Available at www.protective-behaviours.org.au, accessed on 13 February 2016.

Rickard, J. (1996) *Relaxation for Children.* Melbourne, VIC: ACER Press Ltd.

Rosen, M. (1989) *We're Going on a Bear Hunt.* London: Walker Books Ltd.

Schonveld, A. and Myko, V. (1999) *Take Care. Safety Awareness and Personal Safety Issues in the Primary Curriculum.* London: NSPCC.

Schwartz, L. (1979) *Marvellous Me. Creative Activities to Help Develop Self Awareness.* USA: The Learning Works.

Sullivan, P. and Knutson, J. (2000) 'Maltreatment and disabilities: A population based epidemiological study.' *Child Abuse and Neglect 24,* 10, 1257–1273.

Sunderland, M. (2006) *The Science of Parenting.* London: Dorling Kindersley.

Tait, A. and Wosu, H. (2013) *Direct Work with Vulnerable Children.* London: Jessica Kingsley Publishers.

The Lucy Faithfull Foundation (no date) *What's the Problem? A Guide for Parents of Children and Young People Who Have Got into Trouble Online.* Epsom: The Lucy Faithfull Foundation. Available at www.parentsprotect.co.uk/files/Parents%20 Pack_Whats%20the%20problem_11Mar2015.pdf, accessed on 3 March 2016.

Tomlinson, J. (2008) *The Owl Who Was Afraid of the Dark.* London: Egmont.

Veeken, J. (2012) *The Bear Cards: Feelings.* Q Cards. Victoria, Australia. www.qcards. com.au

Wallis, C. and Dell, K. (2004) 'What makes teens tick; A flood of hormones, sure. But also a host of structural changes in the brain. Can those explain the behaviors that make adolescence so exciting – and so exasperating?' *Time Magazine,* 10 May.

Weinberger, D.R, Elvevåg, B. and Giedd, J.N. (2005) *The Adolescent Brain: A Work in Progress.* June. Washington, DC: The National Campaign to Prevent Teen Pregnancy.

Werner, E.E. and Smith, R.S (2001) *Journeys from Childhood to Midlife: Risk, Resilience and Recovery.* Ithaca, NY: Cornell University Press.

Wrench, K. and Naylor, L. (2013) *Life Story Work with Children Who Are Fostered or Adopted. Creative Ideas and Activities.* London: Jessica Kingsley Publishers.

Index